P-51 MUSTANG
vs
Fw 190

Europe 1943–45

MARTIN BOWMAN

First published in Great Britain in 2007 by Osprey Publishing,
Midland House, West Way, Botley, Oxford OX2 0PH, UK
443 Park Avenue South, New York, NY 10016, USA

E-mail: info@ospreypublishing.com

A CIP catalogue record for this book is available from the British Library

ISBN: 978 1 84603 189 2

Edited by Tony Holmes
Cover artwork, three-views and cockpit and armament scrap views by Jim Laurier
Battlescene by Mark Postlethwaite
Index by Alan Thatcher
Typeset in Adobe Garamond and ITC Conduit
Maps by Bounford.com, Huntingdon, UK
Originated by PDQ Digital Media Solutions
Printed in China through Bookbuilders

08 09 10 11 12   13 12 11 10 9 8 7 6 5 4

FOR A CATALOGUE OF ALL BOOKS PUBLISHED BY OSPREY MILITARY
AND AVIATION PLEASE CONTACT:

NORTH AMERICA

Osprey Direct, c/o Random House Distribution Center,
300 Hahn Road, Westminster, MD 21157, USA
E-mail: info@ospreydirect.com

ALL OTHER REGIONS

Osprey Direct UK, PO Box 140 Wellingborough, Northants, NN8 2FA, UK
E-mail: info@ospreydirect.co.uk

www.ospreypublishing.com

Fw 190A cover art
Ltn Klaus Bretschneider, *Staffelkapitän* of 5.(Sturm)/
JG 300, uses his heavily armed Fw 190A-8/R2 to seriously
damage a P-51D from the 352nd FS/353rd FG south-east
of Göttingen on the morning of 27 September 1944.
A Knight's Cross winner, Bretschneider claimed two
P-51s in his tally of 31 victories. He was killed in action
fighting yet more Mustangs on 24 December 1944.
(Artwork by Jim Laurier)

P-51D cover art
1Lt Arthur Cundy of the 353rd FG's 352nd FS guns
down an Fw 190A-8/R2 from JG 4 south-west of
Dummer Lake on 14 January 1945. This aircraft was the
first of three Focke-Wulf fighters to be destroyed by the
20-year-old Floridian, who had scored six victories (all
fighters) to his credit by the time he perished when this
very P-51D crashed into the North Sea after it had
suffered engine failure on 11 March 1945. (Artwork
by Jim Laurier)

GERMAN RANKS	US EQUIVALENT
Reischsmarschall	no equivalent
Generalfeldmarschall	General (five star)
Generaloberst	General (four star)
General der Flieger	Lieutenant General
Generalleutnant	Major or General
Generalmajor	Brigadier General
Oberst	Colonel
Oberstleutnant (Obstlt)	Lieutenant Colonel
Major	Major
Hauptmann (Hptm)	Captain
Oberleutnant (Oblt)	1st Lieutenant
Leutnant (Ltn)	2nd Lieutenant
Stabsfeldwebel (StFw)	Warrant Officer
Oberfähnrich (Ofhr)	no equivalent
Oberfeldwebel (Ofw)	Master Sergeant
Fähnrich (Fhr)	Officer candidate
Feldwebel (Fw)	Technical Sergeant
Unteroffizier (Uffz)	Staff Sergeant
Hauptgefreiter (Hgfr)	Sergeant
Obergefreiter (Ogfr)	Corporal
Gefreiter (Gefr)	Private First Class
Flieger (Flg)	Private Second Class

CONTENTS

INTRODUCTION

The legendary P-51 Mustang, the finest American fighter of World War II, versus the Fw 190A, one of Germany's greatest piston-engined interceptors, provided some of the most deadly combat confrontations of the war in Europe. Combining the endless power of the Packard Merlin with a beautifully designed airframe, the Mustang epitomized the might of the Eighth Air Force's VIII Fighter Command in the final 18 months of the conflict. More than 80 pilots became aces flying the classic North American fighter, a fact that bears testimony to its overall superiority in combat.

Not only was the Mustang capable of meeting the Bf 109G/K and Fw 190A on even or better terms, it could escort the four-engined bombers of VIII Bomber Command on deep penetration missions to their targets and back again. Also, the Mustang's long range gave it an extra dimension by permitting fighter groups to break away and strafe enemy airfields and other targets before returning home.

The rapid improvement and success of the Mustang is even more remarkable when one considers that the Fw 190A was the result of design work begun in late 1937, and as such it had a three-year development advantage over the North American design. Furthermore, when the first Allison-engined P-51s appeared, the Mustang still had a lot of catching up to do in order to realize its potential as a multi-gunned fighter.

In 1940, when the British were shopping for a new fighter, the Mustang's original Allison powerplant was not designed to perform at high altitudes, and so the RAF operated the aircraft in great numbers in the ground attack and tactical reconnaissance roles. The Fw 190A, however, had become the scourge of Allied pilots from the moment it had appeared at German airfields in Belgium in August 1941. A nimble, fast and well-armed adversary, it was technically superior to all British and American fighters in frontline service at that time. This situation only changed with the advent of the Merlin-engined P-51B in late 1943.

In the autumn of 1942, plans had been laid to develop the Mustang as a long-range fighter, fitted with the Rolls-Royce Merlin engine. After overcoming early teething troubles, the worst of which was persistent gun jamming, the P-51B clearly demonstrated its tremendous potential. By early 1944 the aircraft had surpassed the Fw 190A in terms of performance, the latter aircraft's top speed being almost 50mph slower at all heights and 70 mph slower above 28,000ft. There was little to choose between the two when it came to maximum rate of climb, while the Mustang could always out-dive the Fw 190A. Again, in the turning circle both were closely matched, and if anything the Mustang was slightly better. However, not even a Mustang could approach the Fw 190A's outstanding rate of roll. Revisions in design and armament followed, and the P-51D/K became the best of the wartime Mustang breed.

Capable of outperforming German propeller-driven fighters, and able to operate far over the continent with the aid of drop tanks, the P-51D/K was the most successful of all the models to see service in World War II. It was also built in greater quantities than any other variant. In the right hands, the Mustang was superior to the Fw 190A, despite Focke-Wulf trying to keep pace with the Allied fighter through the production of a profusion of newer models that boasted technological innovations such as water/methanol fuel injection to boost engine power for short periods. Ultimately, these improvements were too little, too late.

By late 1944, an average of three German fighters and two pilots were lost for every B-17 or B-24 shot down. The Jagdwaffe was hampered by a lack of fuel, diminishing spares and pilot attrition, and high-scoring Fw 190 *experten* like "Pips" Priller and Heinz Bär and the handful of Focke-Wulf-equipped *Jagdgeschwader* could not overcome the overwhelming odds stacked against them in the defense of the Reich.

This impressive line-up photograph was taken at Debden on 16 June 1944. The P-51B/Cs of the 486th FS/352nd FG had flown south from their base at Bodney to the home of the 4th FG in preparation for the first "Shuttle Mission" to the USSR, but bad weather had caused the operation to be postponed. Codenamed Operation *Frantic*, Shuttle missions were an abortive attempt by the Americans to cooperate with the Soviet forces in the east. The shuttle-bombing program saw the Eighth Air Force's heavy bombers, escorted by Mustangs, hitting targets in eastern Germany and then continuing on to land at Russian bases. The first *Frantic* missions were flown in late June 1944, and the operation proved to be of minimal success. (USAF Museum)

CHRONOLOGY

1937

Autumn   *Reichsluftfahrtministerium* (RLM) places a development contract with Focke-Wulf Flugzeugbau GmbH for a single-seat interceptor fighter to supplement the Messerschmitt Bf 109. Work on the project begins late in 1937 under the direction of Diplom-Ingenieur Kurt Tank.

1938

Summer   Radial-engined design chosen and detailed work on the Fw 190 commences.

1939

June 1   First prototype Fw 190 V1 flies.

1940

April   British Purchasing Commission contracts North American to create an advanced fighter to supplant the Spitfire in RAF service.

Oct 26   Prototype NA-73X flown.

1941

March   After early trials at *Erprobungsstelle* Rechlin, JG 26 begins the task of introducing the Fw 190 into service.

April 23   First NA-73 production aircraft flown.

Fw 190As take shape in Focke-Wulf's Bremen works in 1942–43. [Focke-Wulf, Bremen]

August   First Fw 190A-1s issued to 6./JG 26.

Sept 18   RAF Spitfires and Fw 190s meet in combat for the first time.

1942

Early   Ten factories now building more than 250 Fw 190s monthly.

Feb 23   Eighth Air Force arrives in England.

August 17   First American heavy bomber raid from England.

Oct 13   Rolls-Royce Merlin-powered Mustang flies.

Nov 30   XP-51B, the first Merlin-powered Mustang built in the USA, flies.

1943

Jan 27   First US bombing attack on Germany.

May   Half the Jagdwaffe is equipped with the Fw 190A.

June 22   First really deep USAAF bomber penetration of Germany, to Hüls, near Recklinghausen, on the edge of the Ruhr.

August 17   B-17s bomb Schweinfurt ball-bearing plant and aircraft factories at Regensburg and are engaged by more than 300 fighters put up by 11 Fw 190 *gruppen*. Sixty B-17s are shot down.

Oct 14   Second Schweinfurt raid. Fw 190A-5/R6s of JG 1 and JG 26 feature prominently, and a further 60 B-17s are lost and 138 damaged.

November   First deliveries of P-51Bs to the tactical Ninth Air Force's 354th FG begin.

Nov 17   First flight of the "bubbletop" XP-51D.

Dec 1   P-51Bs from the 354th FG fly their first mission – a sweep over Belgium.

Dec 13   Mustangs fitted with two 92 US gallon internal wing tanks and either two 75-gallon or 150-gallon external tanks fly their first long-range escort mission

P-51B Mustangs (and B-25Hs) crowd the flightline at North American's Mines Field, California, facility in 1944. (North American)

– 490 miles to Kiel and back, which establishes a record at the time.

Dec 16 P-51Bs and Fw 190s engage each other for the first time during a 354th FG escort mission for bombers sent to attack targets in Bremen. No victories claimed by either side.

1944

Jan 1 US Strategic Air Forces in Europe Command established to control the Eighth and Fifteenth Air Forces.

Jan 11 First two Fw 190s to be downed by the P-51B are claimed by the 354th FG's Maj James Howard and 1Lt Jack Bradley.

Jan 24 First two P-51Bs (from the 354th FG) shot down by Fw 190A-7/R2s are claimed by Ofw Rudolf Haninger and Ogfr Krames from 4./JG 1.

Feb 11 357th FG flies its first Mustang escort mission. Originally assigned to the Ninth Air Force, and equipped with P-51Bs, the 357th was transferred to the Eighth Air Force in exchange for the P-47-equipped 358th FG, as VIII Bomber Command desperately needed long-range fighter escorts.

Feb 19–26 "Big Week" series of sustained bombing raids on German aircraft industry.

March P-51D starts to replace the B-model in production. P-51Bs escort bombers to Berlin and back again for the first time.

March 4–6 B-17s become the first US bombers to attack Berlin.

June 6 Operation *Overlord* sees the invasion of northwest France. VIII Fighter Command flies 1,880 sorties and claims 28 enemy fighters shot down. Only two fighters oppose the Allied invasion (Fw 190A-8s from JG 26).

July 7 Fw 190A-8/R2s of IV.(*Sturm*)/JG 3 bring down 12 Eighth Air Force B-24s in a single attack.

September 14 P-51 groups are serving with VIII Fighter Command, as well as three with the Ninth Air Force.

1945

Jan 1 Many Fw 190As lost during Operation *Bodenplatte* (214 Jagdwaffe pilots listed as killed or missing in the wake of this disastrous mission, which sees numerous Allied airfields in western Europe attacked).

April 17 Last P-51 downed by an Fw 190 is claimed west of Prague by leading *Schlacht* ace (with 116 kills) Oblt August Lambert of Schlachtgruppen 77.

May 1 III./JG 51's Fw 190As fly some of the last German fighter missions of the war.

Fw 190A-8 "Yellow 9," probably of *Stab* JG 6, sits with its back broken at Reichenberg airfield in May 1945, having almost certainly been destroyed in a strafing attack by marauding VIII Fighter Command Mustangs. (JaPo courtesy of Theo Boiten)

DESIGN AND DEVELOPMENT

P-51 MUSTANG

In April 1940 British Purchasing Commission (BPC) officials visiting America sought a new long-range fighter to supplement the Spitfire and Hurricane. When they approached North American Aircraft with an invitation to produce the Curtiss 11-87 (P-40D) in quantity under license for the Royal Air Force (RAF), the California-based company suggested instead that it build a brand new and infinitely superior fighter using the same 1,150hp Allison V-1710-39 engine. The BPC accepted the proposal, but a 120-day limit for the construction of a prototype was imposed.

North American's only previous experience in fighter design and construction was limited to the near-identical NA-50 and NA-68, both of which were little more than reworked, single-seat trainers fitted with guns in the wings. Just 13 examples of these aircraft had been built for the Peruvian and Royal Siam air forces in 1939. Nevertheless, North American Aircraft Company president I. H. 'Dutch' Kindelberger was confident that his company could produce an aircraft that answered the needs of the RAF. He and his team of engineers had studied early accounts of air combat in Europe, and these had influenced the design of a new fighter that North American already had on its drawing board prior to the BPC visit. Much useful technical data was also obtained from the Curtiss-Wright Corporation.

With the BPC contract signed, the design team, headed by Lee Atwood, Raymond Rice and German-born Austrian Edgar Schmued (the latter having previously been employed by Dutch aircraft manufacturer Fokker) hastily began work on the new fighter, which was designated the NA-73X – '73' was North American's model number and 'X' denoted its experimental status.

The NA-73X prototype was assembled in 117 days, although when the aircraft was rolled out of the company's Mines Field facility its 1,100hp Allison V-1710-39 (F3R) engine was not yet installed and the prototype was fitted with wheels borrowed from an AT-6 basic trainer. The NA-73 was one of the first fighters to employ a low, square-cut laminar-flow airfoil, which had its maximum thickness well aft. The aircraft duly boasted the lowest-drag wing fitted to any fighter yet built. Drag was further reduced by streamlining a radiator scoop into the underside of the fuselage behind the pilot, whilst keeping the fuselage cross-section to the least depth possible.

On May 4, 1940, the US Army released the new design for sale to Britain, provided that two of the initial batch of fighters be transferred to the US Army Air Corps (USAAC) for tests. After 320 NA-73s were ordered by the BPC 19 days later, the fourth and tenth aircraft were allotted the Army Air Corps designation XP-51 in a contract approved on September, 20. Four days later the BPC increased its purchase to 620 examples. After several modifications, the NA-73X was flown for the first time on October 26, 1940. It crashed on November, 30 following an engine failure in flight, but production was by then assured. Christened the Mustang I by the British, the first production standard aircraft was flown on April, 23 1941 and retained by the company for further testing.

The USAAC's first XP-51 arrived at Wright Field for service testing on August 24, 1941, while the second aircraft was accepted by RAF representatives in September and then sent on a long journey by ship to Liverpool, where it arrived on October 24. Tests soon showed the Mustang I to be superior to the Kittyhawk, Airacobra and Spitfire in both speed and maneuverability at low altitudes. Top speed went from

This P-51B-5 of the 355th FS/354th FG was one of the first Mustangs to venture into the skies of occupied Europe with the "Pioneer Mustang Group" in December 1943. Note the bomb symbols beneath the cockpit, each one denoting a successfully completed escort mission. (USAF)

OPPOSITE
P-51K-5 Mustang 44-11622
flown by Maj Leonard "Kit"
Carson of the 362nd FS/
357th FG, based at Leiston,
Suffolk, in December 1944.

328mph at 1,000ft to 382mph at 13,000ft. Equipment included armor, leak-proof fuel tanks, two 0.50-cal machine guns – with 400 rounds per gun (rpg) – placed low in the nose and two more in the wings, inboard of four 0.30cal weapons with 500rpg.

The first production model destined for RAF service made its maiden flight on May 1, 1941, and a lend-lease contract approved on September 25 that same year added a further 150 Mustang IAs to the production order. These aircraft were armed with four 20mm cannon in the wings, with 125rpg. The first 20 P-51s to follow the last Mustang IAs off the line in July 1942 were taken on charge by the US Army Air Force (USAAF), fitted with two cameras for tactical reconnaissance duties and redesignated F-6As. When this contract was completed two months later, the RAF had received 93 Mustang IAs and the USAAF 55 F-6A photo-reconnaissance aircraft. Two airframes were diverted to the XP-78 project.

The Allison powerplant was not designed to perform at high altitude, so the British decided to operate the Mustang in the armed tactical reconnaissance role with a camera fitted behind the pilot. Although restricted to ceilings below 16,000ft, the Mustang I's speed of almost 353mph at 8,000ft made it ideal for ground attack and tactical reconnaissance, and it began replacing the Curtiss Tomahawk in 11 UK-based Army Cooperation squadrons in the spring of 1942 – the North American machine was also issued to 12 other units. Its first operational sortie was flown on July 27 and in October Allison-powered Mustangs became the first RAF single-engined single-seat fighters to penetrate German airspace from England.

In the autumn of 1942, Maj Thomas Hitchcock (who was later killed flying a Mustang), then assistant air attaché in the US Embassy in London, suggested to senior officers in the USAAF that the Mustang could easily be developed into a long-range fighter through the fitment of the battle-tested Rolls-Royce Merlin engine. Hitchcock reported that the P-51 was one of the best (if not *the* best) fighter airframes developed to date, and advised that it be modified into a high-altitude fighter by "cross-breeding" it with the Merlin 61 engine, which produced a top speed of 400mph at 30,000ft.

America's ranking World War I ace, Eddie Rickenbacker, endorsed Hitchcock's proposal, as did Air Marshal Sir Trafford Leigh-Mallory (then head of the RAF's No 11 Group, and soon to be placed in charge of Fighter Command). Five Mustang Is were subsequently delivered to Rolls-Royce for conversion into Mustang Xs through the fitment of a Merlin 65 to each airframe. At the same time the two surplus Mustang IAs retained by North American in California were modified to take license-built Packard Merlin engines in place of their Allison powerplants. Initially designated the XP-78, the aircraft had become the XP-51B by the time the first example completed its maiden flight on November 30, 1942.

A little over 12 months later, the Packard Merlin Mustang would start to provide the answer to the USAAF's prayers for a long range fighter capable of escorting its heavy bombers to and from heavily defended targets in occupied Europe and "fortress Germany" itself. And although the marriage between the American airframe and the British engine went remarkably smoothly, the new P-51B was still beset with other technical problems that initially nullified its abilities in combat. Its engine routinely suffered from coolant loss at high altitude during the course of long escort missions,

P-51K-5 MUSTANG

32ft 3in

12ft 2in

37ft 0in

resulting in overheating and eventually failing powerplants. Oil leaks also plagued early-build P-51Bs, and the fighter's oxygen system struggled to cope with four- to five-hour sorties that were the norm in the ETO.

Although these problems were serious enough, gun stoppages in combat drew the most criticism from pilots flying the B-model Mustang in combat in 1943–44. The P-51B was fitted with just four 0.50-cal machine guns – two in each wing. Its laminar airfoil section was too thin to accommodate the weapons in the normal upright position, so they were canted over about 30 degrees. Thus, the ammunition feed trays had to curve slightly upward and then down again to enable link-belted rounds to enter the gun at the right angle. Gun jams were almost inevitable if the weapons were fired while the pilot was maneuvering at anything beyond 1.5g.

Numerous modifications were made both by the manufacturer and units in the field in an effort to solve the gun jams. An example of the latter saw an enterprising groundcrewman from the 354th FG obtain some electric ammunition feed motors that were being used in the Martin B-26 Marauder to carry shells from the ammunition boxes to the guns in the medium bomber. Once fitted to the P-51Bs, these seemed to go a long way to eradicating the jamming problem.

Capt Bill Whisner claimed 14.5 aerial victories in the Mustang in 1944–45 flying with the 352nd FG's 487th FS. His first Fw 190 victories were scored in the P-51B, and he recalled some of the technical issues that beset the early model Mustang;

Our first B-models did have some teething problems that needed to be worked out. The Packard Merlin engine had numerous difficulties with its coolant, oil, fuel and electrical systems. Our guns were also a continual source of frustration. Any time we pulled more than 1.5 to 2gs they would jam, usually because rounds would fail to eject from the belt. Some stopgap measures were undertaken, but the problem was not alleviated until the introduction of the D-model, which had a redesigned gun belt and ammunition feed system. Meanwhile, we had to take our chances with the guns while maneuvering in combat, or confine our firing to straight and level flight! The greenhouse canopy had the disadvantage of restricted visibility, especially to the rear, which was also a real problem in combat.

The P-51B was followed by 1,750 P-51Cs, which were virtually identical to the B-model but built in North American's new Dallas factory. A number of these aircraft were fitted with British-designed Malcolm bulged sliding frameless hoods similar to the Spitfire canopy in the UK, improving the rearward visibility for the pilot. Malcolm hoods were fitted to most RAF Mustang IIIs delivered in 1944, as well as to a number of USAAF P-51B/Cs. By late 1943, a major re-design of the Mustang's fuselage had seen a streamlined "bubble" canopy mated to a cut-down rear fuselage. The definitive P-51D would soon be rolling off the production line in California.

The D-model, powered by the Packard Merlin V-1650-7 and fitted with six 0.50-cal machine guns (400rpg), was a considerably improved machine. Its wing had been thickened slightly so that the six guns could be fitted in an upright position, and this meant no more jams. Other changes less visible to the eye, but of equal or greater importance, included the K-14 100mm fixed-reticule gun sight. This replaced the P-51B/C's optical sight, with its 70mm reticule, which was too small for angle-off shooting. The new gun sight made deflection shooting and range estimation considerably easier. The gun sight consisted principally of a piece of slanted, clear glass centered above the instrument panel directly in the pilot's line of sight. When activated, a center dot of yellow light, known as a "pipper", was projected onto the glass. The "pipper" was in turn surrounded by a circle formed of six or eight diamond-shaped dots. Using the control lever mounted on the throttle handle, the diamonds were expanded or contracted so that they continually "bracketed" the target. This automatically calculated the amount of lead needed for the range of the target, and meant the pilot had an excellent chance of scoring hits.

As previously noted, the Merlin Mustang was powered by a V-1650 engine built under license in the USA by luxury automobile company Packard. The V-1650 could be taken up to 61 inches of manifold pressure at 3,000rpm for take-off or, if needed in combat, 67 inches for up to five minutes in Emergency Power. Normally-aspirated engines tended to run out of power as altitude increased, usually between 15,000ft and

A war-weary P-51B is overhauled at the Eighth Air Force's repair and replacement center at the 3rd Base Air Depot at Warton, in Lancashire, in early 1944. (Courtesy of Dave Mayor)

20,000ft. The Merlin-powered P-51, however, had a two-stage blower in the induction system that was controlled automatically with a barometric switch. At around 17,000ft, when the throttle had been advanced almost all the way forward just to maintain normal cruise, the blower would kick into high, the manifold pressure would jump up and the climb could be continued to 30,000ft. The P-51 could be taken a lot higher than that, but above 30,000ft its engine power began to tail off rapidly and the pilot had to use his controls gingerly in order not to stall the fighter.

The P-51D/K was to become the most successful Mustang variant, being built in greater numbers than any other model – 6,502 were completed at Inglewood, in California, and 1,454 rolled off the Dallas production line. Early on in its production life, the P-5ID/K received a dorsal fin to compensate for the loss of keel surface due to the reduction of rear fuselage decking, and tail warning radar was also added in due course.

The P-51D first saw frontline service in Europe with the Eighth Air Force immediately prior to D-Day. It quickly excelled in high-altitude escort and combat, being superior in both speed and maneuverability to all Luftwaffe piston-engined fighters above 20,000ft. In order to make the most of the aircraft's agility, VIII Fighter Command pilots were among the first to wear anti-g suits, which inflated automatically around their calves, thighs and lower body during tight turns and when pulling out from a dive. The g-suit restricted the blood from draining from the head and trunk, and thus delayed the onset of "black-out." The only slight drawback associated with this new flying apparel was that pilots found they could then take more "g" than their P-51s, and Mustangs would regularly land following combat with deformed wings and numerous popped rivets.

When production of the P-51D ended in August 1945, the total number of Mustangs completed stood at 15,484, with 5,541 of these aircraft in frontline service with the USAAF at war's end.

Fw 190

In late 1937, a development contract was issued to Focke-Wulf Flugzeugbau GmbH for a single-seat interceptor fighter to supplement the Messerschmitt Bf 109. Under Kurt Tank's direction, a design team led by Oberingenieur Blaser created a low-wing monoplane with a fully retractable undercarriage that could be powered by either the Daimler-Benz DB 601 12-cylinder vee liquid-cooled inline engine (as fitted to the Bf 109) or the BMW 139 18-cylinder two-row radial.

A radial engine typically causes drag and is bulky, and the latter trait reduces the pilot's forward visibility during take-off and landing. However, the Reichsluftfahrministerium (RLM) surprisingly ordered the radial-engined fighter to be developed so as not to overburden Daimler-Benz – a decision which amazed Tank and his colleagues. Detailed work on the fighter began the following summer.

Flugkapitän Hans Sander, in his capacity as Focke-Wulf's chief test pilot, flew the first prototype from the company's Bremen facility on June 1, 1939. It was powered by a fan-cooled 1,550hp BMW 139 radial which was fitted with a special ducted spinner to reduce drag. After five test flights, the aircraft was transferred to Rechlin, where a speed of 595kmh (370mph) was achieved. During October 1939 a second prototype was completed, this machine being fitted with two 13mm MG 131 and 7.9mm MG 17 machine guns.

In June 1939 the BMW 139 engine was abandoned and work began on the 14-cylinder BMW 801. In an effort to compensate for the greater weight associated with this new engine, the fighter's cockpit was moved farther aft.

Despite its bulky powerplant, the Fw 190 was small, the BMW engine being neatly faired into a slim fuselage. In stark contrast to the Bf 109, the Focke-Wulf fighter was fitted with an extensively glazed cockpit canopy which afforded the pilot with an excellent all-round view.

Early in 1940, Reichsmarschall Hermann Göring visited the Focke-Wulf factory and inspected the Fw 190 V2 second prototype. He was very impressed, and told Tank that he "must turn these new fighters out like so many hot rolls!"

The success of the BMW 801-engined aircraft led to the construction of 30 pre-production machines, designated Fw 190A-0, and 100 Fw 190A-1 production models were also subsequently ordered. Early trials were carried out at Erprobungsstelle Rechlin, and in March 1941 pilots and engineers from JG 26 prepared to introduce the new fighter into Luftwaffe service. In August the first Fw 190A-1s were delivered to 6./JG 26 at Le Bourget.

On September 18, when RAF Spitfire Vs and Fw 190s clashed for the first time, it soon became obvious that the German fighter was more maneuverable in almost every respect, and also possessed a higher maximum speed. Fw 190As fought their first major action in early February 1942, when they were among the fighters used to cover the battlecruisers *Scharnhorst* and *Gneisenau* and the heavy cruiser *Prinz Eugen* as they sailed from Brest to the safety of north German ports. Jagdwaffe fighters fought off British attempts to destroy the ships, and Fw 190A-1s from III./JG 26 shot down six Swordfish torpedo-bombers.

A BMW 801D-2 installation in an Fw 190A. The whole powerplant arrangement was neat and closely cowled – undoubtedly one of the finest examples of radial engine installation in World War II. (Focke-Wulf, Bremen)

Orders soon followed for the improved Fw 190A-2, which was powered by the BMW 801C-2 engine and armed with two 7.9mm MG 17 machine guns above the engine cowling and two 20mm MG FF cannon in the wing roots – the aircraft also often carried an extra pair of MG 17 guns in the outer wings. The A-2 was followed by the Fw 190A-3, which was powered by a 1,700hp BMW 80ID-2 engine and had the MG FF cannon moved outboard and replaced by two of the much faster firing 20mm MG 151/20 cannon. The cockpit canopy could be jettisoned with the aid of explosive bolts and the pilot was protected by 8mm and 14mm armor plating. By early 1942 more than 250 Fw 190s were being produced every month. In March 1942 II./JG 26, which was often in the forefront of attacks on American day bombers and their fighter escorts, was re-equipped with the Fw 190A-3. In April JG 2 was also equipped with the Fw 190A-3 in the west. Four months later the Fw 190A-4, powered by the BMW 80ID-2 engine (fitted with water-methanol injection that provided 2,100hp for short periods), entered production.

Although the Fw 190A had proven itself to be an extremely effective fighter, operational experience revealed that the power of the BMW 801 engine tended to drop off at altitudes in excess of 7,000m (22,967ft). Attempts were therefore made to improve the high altitude performance of the aircraft during the subsequent production of Fw 190A, B and C variants.

In June 1942 Fw 190s were issued to JG 1 to combat American bomber formations appearing over the Reich, as well as to IV./JG 5 in Norway. The following month the first Spitfire IXs entered RAF service, and these aircraft met the Fw 190 on almost equal terms. However, on August 19, when the Fw 190s went into action against Allied fighters and landing craft during the ill-fated Dieppe operation, the RAF lost 106 aircraft, of which JG 2 and JG 26 claimed the lion's share. By the end of the year, with the American daylight bombing raids increasing in their intensity, several more Luftwaffe Gruppen were equipped with the Fw 190.

Early in 1943 the Fw 190A-5, which was essentially similar to the A-4, appeared. This version differed from its predecessor by having a revised engine mounting to allow the BMW 801D-2 to be fitted 15cm (5.9inches) farther forward of the cockpit. This arrangement was designed to eliminate engine overheating problems which had consistently plagued the aircraft since its service introduction almost two years earlier.

By the start of 1943, the Eighth Air Force in East Anglia had became a potent threat, conducting raids on targets in the Reich. The situation had become so serious by July that Luftwaffe fighter units had to be transferred to airfields in the west from the eastern front and the Mediterranean. From late August 1943 onwards, six Jagdgruppen equipped with Fw 190A-4/5s were available for operations against the Allied air forces flying from Britain. On August 17, when the Eighth Air Force attacked Regensburg and Schweinfurt, more than 300 Fw 190s met the four-engined bombers. The Americans lost 60 "heavies," with almost all of them falling to German fighters. On October 14, when the Eighth Air Force attacked ball-bearing factories in Schweinfurt, Fw 190A-5/R6 fighters shot down a high proportion of the 79 bombers that were destroyed. A further 120 "heavies" were damaged.

Fw 190A-8

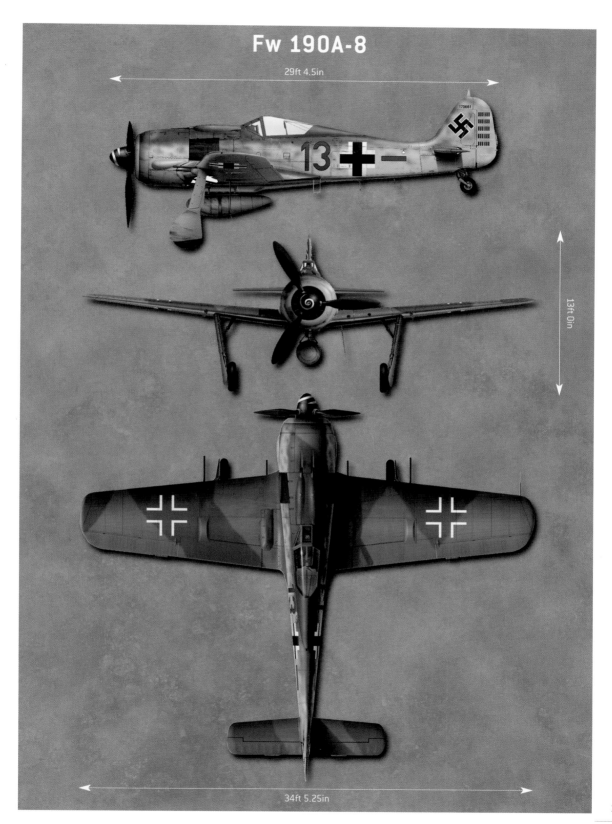

29ft 4.5in

13ft 0in

34ft 5.25in

The next major variant of the Focke-Wulf to enter service was the Fw 190A-6, which had a redesigned wing that was both lighter and could carry four 20mm MG 151/20 cannon – two MG 17 machine guns were also mounted above the engine. The A-6/R1 carried six 20mm MG 151/20 cannon and the Fw 190A-6/R3 two 30mm MK 103 cannon in underwing gondolas. In December 1943 the Fw 190A-7 entered production.

The final large-scale production version of the A-series was the Fw 190A-8, fitted with an additional 115-litre internal fuel tank and other refinements. One of the last production variants of the A-series was the Fw 190A-9, which was similar to the A-8 but was powered by a 2,000hp BMW 801F engine. Although the radial-engined Fw 190A series was the principal variant to see service with the Luftwaffe, thousands of Fw 190F/Gs eventually replaced the Ju 87 Stuka as Germany's chief close-support aircraft. Essentially these planes were ground-attack versions of the basic Fw 190A series serving as fighter-bombers. Due to their ground-attack roles neither variant can be regarded as a direct opponent of the Merlin-engined P-51.

As good as the BMW-radial engined Fw 190A was, its performance fell away badly at high altitudes. It would struggle to be a premier air superiority fighter once the P-51D appeared in the ETO from June 1944. Following two years of development, the first of some 700 Junkers Jumo 213 inline-engined Fw 190D-9s began pouring off the Cottbus assembly line in August 1944. Although a match for the P-51D, the "Dora-9" was only ever considered 'an emergency solution' by chief designer Tank, whose ultimate high-altitude fighter was the inline-engined Ta 152H. Also built at Cottbus, production examples of the Ta 152H started to leave the Focke-Wulf plant in November 1944, and by the time the factory was abandoned in early 1945, 150 examples had been delivered to the Luftwaffe. Most of these aircraft were issued to JG 301. Although the Fw 190D-9 and Ta 152H were clearly better air superiority fighters, their paucity in numbers meant that the radial-engined Fw 190A series machines remained in the vanguard of Jagdwaffe through to VE-Day, opposing the thousands of Mustangs that ruled German skies in the last year of the war.

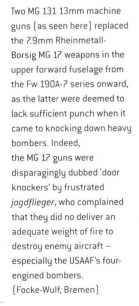

Two MG 131 13mm machine guns (as seen here) replaced the 7.9mm Rheinmetall-Borsig MG 17 weapons in the upper forward fuselage from the Fw 190A-7 series onward, as the latter were deemed to lack sufficient punch when it came to knocking down heavy bombers. Indeed, the MG 17 guns were disparagingly dubbed 'door knockers' by frustrated *jagdflieger*, who complained that they did no deliver an adequate weight of fire to destroy enemy aircraft – especially the USAAF's four-engined bombers. (Focke-Wulf, Bremen)

TECHNICAL SPECIFICATIONS

P-51

MUSTANG I

Limitations with the Allison engine, whose power fell off dramatically above 12,000ft, resulted in the powerplant proving unsuitable for combat and interception roles in Europe, where fighter-versus-fighter engagements often took place at altitudes in excess of 20,000ft. Instead, the aircraft was used for tactical reconnaissance, armed with four 0.50-in and four 0.303-in machine guns, which were used to good effect in the ground attack role. RAF Mustang Is equipped with an obliquely-mounted camera served with no fewer than 23 squadrons of Army Co-operation Command. A further 300 generally similar aircraft followed, the RAF receiving 93 examples (Mustang IA). These differed from the earlier model in having self-sealing fuel tanks and four 20mm cannon – the latter fitted in the wings. Some 55 camera-equipped F-6A aircraft were used by the USAAF for tactical reconnaissance.

A-36A

RAF operation of the Mustang in the ground-attack role saw the USAAF procure 500 aircraft, which were called Apaches. These aircraft were fitted with dive brakes and underwing bomb racks. One A-36A was supplied to the RAF.

P-51A

The USAAF procured 310 examples powered by the 1,200hp V-1710-81 engine with war-emergency boost. Armament consisted of four 0.50-in machine guns with 1,260 rounds, and two 500lb bombs or drop tanks could be carried on underwing racks. Fifty P-51As were allocated to the RAF as Mustang IIs, and 35 were converted into camera-equipped tactical reconnaissance F-6B aircraft for the USAAF.

P-51B

For evaluation purposes, two P-51As (later redesignated XP-78 and finally XP-51B) were powered by Packard-built Merlin V-1650-3 engines and two-stage superchargers rated by the USAAF at 1,295hp at 28,750ft, with 1,595hp available as a war-emergency boost setting up to 17,000ft. The XP-51Bs attained a maximum speed of 441mph at 29,800ft. The first Merlin-engined Mustang built in the USA flew on November 30, 1942, with a four-bladed Hamilton propeller and the carburetor intake below, instead of above, the engine.

The first P-51B-1-NA was flown on May 5, 1943. Armament still consisted of four 0.50-in machine guns – half the armament of the P-47 – but the 440mph top speed was the fastest among fighters then in combat. An 85-gallon fuel tank was fitted behind the cockpit, and together with two 108- or 150-gallon drop tanks under the wings, the Mustang had the range to accompany bombers to any target in Germany. A total of 1,988 B-models were built at Inglewood, the last 550 becoming P-51B-7s to -10s. The addition of an 85-gallon fuselage fuel tank increased the fighter's total internal fuel capacity to 269 US gallons and the normal range to 1,300 miles. This modification was also made in the field to earlier P-51B/Cs. Some 274 P-51Bs were allocated to the RAF as Mustang IIIs.

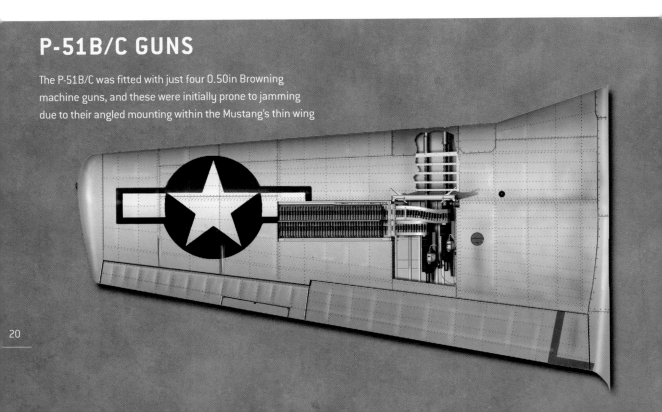

P-51B/C GUNS

The P-51B/C was fitted with just four 0.50in Browning machine guns, and these were initially prone to jamming due to their angled mounting within the Mustang's thin wing

Armorers from the 374th FS/ 361st FG carefully feed belted 0.50-in API rounds into ammunition trays on the grass at the group's Bottisham base in June 1944. Note the fresh, prominent, D-Day invasion stripes on the P-51Bs behind them. (National Archives)

P-51C

Generally similar to the P-51B, 1,750 C-models were built at North American's new Dallas plant. Both the B- and C-models differed from earlier versions by having a strengthened fuselage and redesigned ailerons, and they were initially powered by the Packard Merlin V-1650-3, followed by the V-1650-7 Merlin 68. The latter had a war emergency rating of 1,695hp at 10,300ft, and produced a maximum speed of 439mph

P-51D/K GUNS

The P-51D/K was fitted with six 0.50in Browning machine guns, and these proved to be far more reliable than the weapons in the early-model Merlin Mustangs

thanks to their upright mounting in the fighter's slightly deeper wings

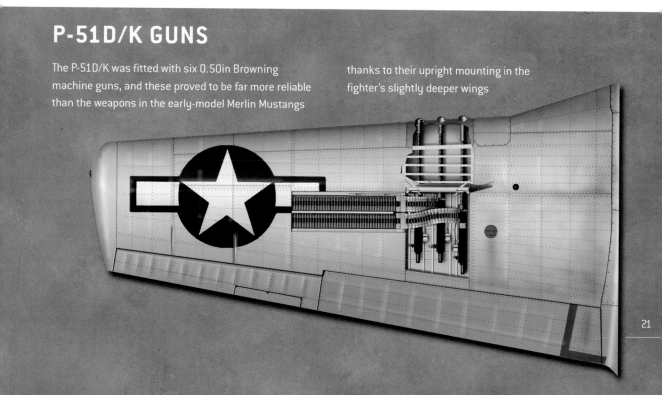

at 25,000ft. The sea-level climb rate was 3,900ft/min. Maximum weight with a 2,000lb bomb load was 11,200lb. Armament was four 0.50-in machine guns in the wings, with a total of 1,260 rounds of ammunition. The RAF received 636 P-51Cs (Mustang IIIs). 71 USAAF P-51B/Cs were modified as F-6C tactical reconnaissance aircraft.

P-51D

The major production version, with a total of 7,956 built, the D-model introduced the bubble canopy to improve the pilot's field of view, a modified rear fuselage and six 0.50-in machine guns. Fifty P-51Ds were supplied to the nationalist Chinese Air Force and 40 to the Royal Netherlands Air Force in the PTO. A modification of this series resulted in ten TP-51D trainers being built with radio equipment relocated and an additional seat, with full dual controls, behind the pilot seat. One TP-51D was further modified for use as a high-speed observation post for the Supreme Allied Commander, Gen Dwight Eisenhower, who flew in it to inspect the Normandy beachheads in June 1944.

F-6D

136 tactical reconnaissance aircraft were modified from the P-51D production contract. 281 were allocated to the RAF (Mustang IV).

P-51K

1,500 generally similar examples differed only in the replacement of the Hamilton-Standard airscrew by an Aeroproduct propeller and a slightly modified canopy with a blunter rear. Weighing 11,000lb loaded, the P-51K was not fitted with rocket stubs, and it had a slightly inferior performance to the P-51D. 163 were completed as F-6K tactical reconnaissance examples. 594 were allocated to the RAF (Mustang IV).

Fw 190A

Fw 190 V1 and V2

The Fw 190 prototype (D-OPZE) was rolled out in May 1939 and flew for the first time from Bremen airfield on June 1. The aircraft was powered by a fan-cooled 1,550hp BMW 139 radial fitted with a special ducted spinner to reduce drag, but the engine overheated rapidly nevertheless, and eventually the ducted spinner was removed and replaced by a new tightly-fitting NACA cowling. Fw 190 V2 second prototype was also fitted with a large ducted spinner and powered by a BMW 139 engine. The latter was subsequently replaced by the longer and heavier BMW 801 powerplant, which necessitated structural changes to the aircraft and the relocation of the cockpit. These prototypes were armed with two 13mm MG 131 machine guns in the wings and two 7.92mm MG 17 weapons in the upper forward fuselage. The third and fourth prototypes were abandoned.

Fw 190 V5/V5g

Once powered by the new 1,660hp BMW 801C-0 engine, the V2 was modified to take a wing of increased span. To compensate for the greater engine weight, the cockpit was moved farther aft. With the introduction of the V5g ('g' standing for gross or large), the V5 short span version (which had a wing area of 15 sq m (161.46 sq ft) was redesignated the Fw 190 V5k ('k' standing for klein or small). The V5k had a wing area of 18.3 sq m (196.98 sq ft).

Fw 190A-0

The pre-production batch, nine of these aircraft were fitted with the small wing, while the remainder had the larger span version. 100 production Fw 190As were ordered, the first five of which bore the alternative designations V7 to V11.

Fw 190A-1

This initial production model was essentially similar to the V5g, being powered by a 1,660hp BMW 801C-1 radial, having the long-span wing and 7.92mm MG 17 machine guns and FuG 7a radio equipment. In August 1941 the first Fw 190A-1s were delivered to *Geschwader-Stab* JG 26, commanded by Obstlt Adolf Galland.

Fw 190A-2

The Fw 190 V14 first prototype had two 7.9mm MG 17 machine guns above the engine cowling and two 20mm MG FF cannon in the wing roots. The production Fw 190A-2, which was powered by the BMW 801C-2 engine, often carried an additional pair of MG 17 guns in the outboard wing panels.

Fw 190A-3

This was the first major production variant, which was powered by the 1,700hp BMW 801D-2 engine. It had the MG FF cannon moved to the outer wing panels, and their original location used instead for two of the much faster firing 20mm

Fw 190A-6s of Sturmstaffel 1, freshly marked with black-white-black Defence of the Reich identification bands, are lined up for a propaganda photograph at Dortmund airfield in January 1944. Note the barrels for the four MG 151 20mm cannon in the wings, and the absence of the previously standard twin MG 131 machine guns immediately forward of the canopy. Having been established in October 1943 with heavily-armored Fw 190A-6s, this special bomber-destroyer unit conducted independent operations against American heavy bomber formations until it was incorporated into IV.(Sturm)/JG 3 in April 1944. (Courtesy of Eddie Creek)

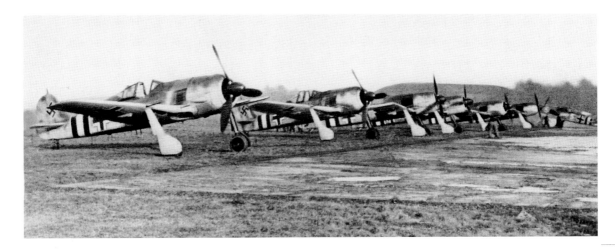

MG 151/20 weapons. The cockpit canopy could be jettisoned with the aid of explosive bolts and the pilot was protected by 8mm and 14mm armor plate. The first examples were introduced into service in autumn 1941.

Fw 190A-4

Delivered during the late summer of 1942 with FuG 16Z radio and a fin-mounted radio mast atop the fin. The BMW 801D-2 engine had provision for MW-50 water/methanol fuel injection to boost output to 2,100hp for short periods, and thus raise the maximum speed to 416mph at 21,000ft.

Fw 190A-4/R6

MW-50 fuel injection deleted. Capable of carrying two underwing *Wurfgranaten* WGr 21 210mm rocket launchers for the unguided WGr 21 *Dodel* missile. Fixed armament was reduced to two MG 151 cannon.

Fw 190A-4/U5

Able to carry a 66-Imperial gallon drop tank beneath each wing and a 1,102lb bomb under the fuselage.

Fw 190A-5

Introduced in early 1943, this version was essentially similar to the A-4 but had a revised engine mounting which enabled the BMW 801D-2 to be fitted 15cm farther forward in an attempt to cure a tendency for the engine to overheat. Many sub-variants were produced.

Fw 190A-7 COWLING GUNS

The Fw 190A-7 boasted two 13mm MG 131 machine guns fitted in the upper forward fuselage, these weapons having replaced 7.9mm Rheinmetall-Borsig MG 17s that had been a feature of all previous Fw 190s

Fw 190A-5/U16

Armed with 30mm MK 108 cannon in the outboard wing position as standard.

Fw 190A-6

Developed from the experimental Fw 190A-5/U10 in June 1943. A redesigned, lighter wing could take four 20mm MG 151/20 cannon whilst retaining the two MG 17 machine guns mounted above the engine. FuG 16ZE and FuG 25 radio equipment was also carried.

Fw 190A-6/R1

Developed following successful trials with the Fw 190A-5/U12, this aircraft had six 20mm MG 151/20 cannon and was used operationally by JG 11.

Fw 190 V51

Forerunner of the A-6/R2, which could carry a 30mm MK 108 in the outboard, wing position.

Fw 190A-6/R3

Armed with two 30mm MK 103 cannon in underwing gondolas.

Fw 190A-6/R4

Was to be fitted with a BMW 801TS engine with a turbo-supercharger. The only prototype (Fw 190 V45) was initially fitted with a BMW 801D-2 engine with GM-1 power-boosting, being re-engined with the BMW 801TS in July 1944.

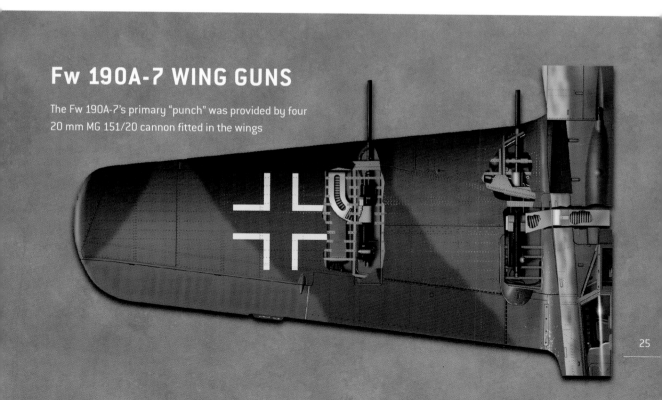

Fw 190A-7 WING GUNS

The Fw 190A-7's primary "punch" was provided by four 20 mm MG 151/20 cannon fitted in the wings

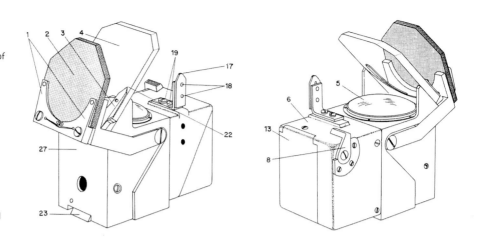

Front and rear three-quarter drawings of the Revi 16B gunsight as fitted to the Fw 190A-7 and later models of the Focke-Wulf fighter, replacing the earlier Revi C12D. It was fitted offset slightly to the right in the Fw 190's cockpit. Important features are the main focusing lens (5) and lens chamber (27), as well as the reflector plate (4) on which the illuminated sighting image was projected when the internal light bulb (inside the housing marked with the number 13) was switched on. The sight could also be used as a simple mechanical "manual" sight, using the rear sighting post (17) and forward post-type projection (22). (Focke-Wulf, Bremen)

Fw 190A-6/R6

The final A-6 variant, this aircraft could carry a 210mm *Wurfgranaten* WGr 21 rocket tube beneath each wing.

Fw 190A-7

Introduced in December 1943, and basically similar to the Fw 190A-6, the first prototype was the Fw 190A-5/U9, which had two MG 151/20 cannon in the wings and two 13mm MG 131 machine guns above the engine cowling. The second prototype (Fw 190 V35) was similar, but had four MG 151/20s in the wings and a strengthened undercarriage. It was later re-engined with a 2,000hp BMW 801F engine, which was also tested in the V36. The *Rüstsatz* (conversion packs) produced for the A-7 was similar to that for the A-6, with much emphasis being placed on the A-7/R6 with *Wurfgranaten* WGr 210cm rocket tubes.

Fw 190A-8/R7

Fitted with an armored cockpit for use by the newly-established anti-bomber *Sturmgruppen*.

Fw 190A-8/R11

All-weather fighter with heated canopy and PKS 12 radio navigation equipment.

OTHER FW 190 VARIANTS:

The following inline-engined variants were excellent air superiority fighters, but saw very limited service.

Fw 190D-9

Powered by the inline 2,000hp Junkers Jumo 213, the "Dora-9" was a match for the P-51D. However, only 700 were ever produced, which meant that it could never hope to rival the Mustang for air superiority.

Ta 152H

Featuring a wider wingspan, stretched fuselage, broad chord fin and a pressurised cockpit, the Ta 152H was powered by the Junkers Jumo 213E engine. Only 150 were ever delivered to the Luftwaffe.

A VIEW FROM THE COCKPIT

Legendary British test pilot Capt Eric Brown flew many German aircraft both during and immediately after World War II. Amongst the types to appear in his logbook was an Fw 190A-4 that had been landed by its pilot in error at the RAF fighter station at West Malling, in Kent, on April, 17 1943. Sent to Farnborough for evaluation three days later, Brown soon got to fly it;

From any angle, in the air or on the ground, the Focke-Wulf was an aerodynamic beauty, and it oozed lethality. It sat high on the ground, and in getting into the cockpit it was immediately evident that the ground view left much to be desired, for the BMW 801D air-cooled radial engine, although beautifully cowled, could not but help be obtrusive. Nevertheless, it still offered a better view forward than was obtainable from the Bf 109, the Spitfire or the Mustang.

The cockpit, while on the narrow side by Allied standards of the day, was fairly comfortable, with a semi-reclining seat for the pilot, which was ideally suited for high-g maneuvers. Contrary to expectations, the flight instruments were not quite so well arranged as those of the Bf 109, but the general layout of the cockpit was good. Perhaps its most novel feature was its ingenious Kommandgerät – "a brain-box" which relieved the pilot of the task of controlling mixture, airscrew pitch, boost and rpm, executing all these functions automatically.

All the ancillary controls were electrically operated by a mass of pushbuttons, which were obviously intended for daintily-gloved fingers and not for the massive leather flying gauntlets issued to British aircrew – the latter converted the human hand into a bunch of bananas.

The most impressive feature of the Focke-Wulf was its beautifully light ailerons and high rate of roll. The ailerons maintained their lightness from the stall up to 400mph, although they became heavier above that speed. At lower speeds the Focke-Wulf tended to tighten up in the turn, and a slight forward pressure on the stick had to be applied. But above that figure the changeover called for some backward pressure to hold the aircraft in the turn. Rudder control was positive and effective at low speeds and satisfactory at high speeds, when it seldom had to be used for any normal maneuver.

It was when one took the three controls together rather than in isolation that one realised that the Fw 190's magic as a fighter lay in its superb harmony of control. To be a good dogfighter, and at the same time a good gun platform, required just those very characteristics that the Focke-Wulf possessed in all important matters of stability and control.

The Focke-Wulf had harsh stalling characteristics, which limited its maneuver margins. I flew several varieties of the breed many times, and each time I experienced that sense of exhilaration that came from flying an aircraft that one instinctively knew to be a top-notcher, but at the same time demanded handling skill if its high qualities were to be exploited.

P-51D/K COCKPIT

1. Landing gear control lever
2. Elevator trim tab control wheel
3. Carburetor hot air control lever
4. Carburetor cold air control lever
5. Rudder trim tab control
6. Aileron trim tab control
7. Coolant radiator control
8. Oil radiator control
9. Landing light switch
10. Florescent light switch, left
11. Flare pistol port cover
12. Arm rest
13. Mixture control lever
14. Throttle quadrant locks
15. Throttle control
16. Propeller pitch control
17. Selector dimmer assembly
18. Instrument light
19. Rear radar warning lamp
20. K-14A gun sight
21. Laminated glass
22. Remote compass indicator
23. Clock
24. Suction gauge
25. Manifold pressure gauge
26. Air speed indicator
27. Directional gyro turn indicator
28. Artificial horizon
29. Coolant temperature
30. Tachometer
31. Altimeter
32. Turn and bank indicator
33. Rate of climb indicator
34. Carburetor temperature
35. Engine temperature gauge
36. Bomb release levers
37. Engine control panel
38. Landing gear indicator lights
39. Parking brake handle
40. Oxygen flow indicator
41. Oxygen pressure gauge
42. Ignition switch
43. Bomb and rocket switch
44. Cockpit light control
45. Rocket control panel
46. Fuel shut-off valve
47. Fuel selector valve
48. Emergency hydraulic release handle
49. Hydraulic pressure gauge
50. Oxygen hose
51. Oxygen regulator
52. Canopy release handle
53. Canopy crank
54. IFF control panel
55. IFF detonator buttons
56. VHF radio control box
57. Rear radar control panel
58. VHF volume control
59. Florescent light switch, right
60. Electrical control panel
61. Circuit breakers
62. BC-438 control box
63. Cockpit light
64. Circuit breakers
65. Rudder pedals
66. Control column
67. Flaps control lever
68. Pilot's seat
69. Flare gun storage

Fw 190A-7 COCKPIT

1 to 4. Controls for FuG 16ZY radio
5. Horizontal stabilizer trim control
6. Undercarriage and flaps controls
7. Horizontal stabilizer trim indicator
8. Landing gear and flaps actuation buttons
9. Throttle and propeller pitch control
10. Instrument panel lighting dimmer control
11. Fuel cock control lever
12. Engine starter brushes cut-off
13 to 15. IFF controls for FuG 25 equipment
16. Landing gear manual extension control
17. Cockpit ventilator

18. Fuel tank selector
19. Altimeter
20. Fuel and pressure gauge
21. Pitot tube heater light
22. Jettison lever for under-fuselage stores
23. Oil temperature gauge
24. Air speed indicator
25 and 26. MG 131 guns armed lights
27. Artificial horizon
28. Armament switches, ammunition counter and armament control unit
29. Revi 16B gun sight
30. Engine cooling flaps control
31. Armored glass windscreen
32. Rate of climb indicator

33. AFN-2 homing indicator for FuG 16ZY
34. Compass
35. Fuel gauge
36. Propeller pitch indicator
37. Engine supercharger pressure gauge
38. Cockpit light
39. Tachometer
40. Fuel low warning light
41. Rear fuel tank switch-over light
42. Fuel tank selector switch
43. Flare gun port
44. Oxygen flow indicator
45. Oxygen pressure gauge
46. Oxygen flow valve
47. Canopy crank
48. Circuit breakers

49. Canopy jettison lever
50. Engine starter switch
51 and 52. Clock
53. Flare gun door jettison button
54. Bomb fuse activator
55. Compass deviation table
56. Fuel pump circuit breaker
57. Flare gun stowage
58. Circuit breaker panel
59. Machine guns' circuit breaker
60. Pilot's seat
61. Control column
62. Wing cannon firing button
63. Bomb release switch
64. Rudder pedals
65. Throttle lever damper control

Four Mustangs from the 361st FG formate shown returning from a bomber escort mission to Munich on July 11, 1944. These fighters are from the 375th FS, with group CO, Col Thomas J J Christian, leading the four-ship in P-51D-5 44-13410 *LOU IV/Athlene*. Christian was killed in this aircraft on August 12, 1944 when it crashed while attacking a marshalling yard near Arras. The second P-51D-5 in the formation is 44-13926, flown by the 361st FG's third-ranking ace, 1Lt Urban Drew. Alongside Drew is 1Lt Bruce Rowlett in his personal Mustang, 44-13568 *Sky Bouncer*, whilst occupying the No 4 slot is soon to be retired P-51B 42-106811 *SUZY G*, flown by Capt Francis Glanker. (Courtesy of Steve Gotts)

Just as the Spitfire IX was probably the most outstanding British fighter aircraft to give service in World War II, its Teutonic counterpart undoubtedly deserves the same recognition for Germany. Both were supreme in their time and their class. Both were durable and technically superb, and if each had not been there to counter the other, then the balance of air power could have been dramatically altered at a crucial period in the fortunes of both combatants.

How did the Mustang match up against the Fw 190A? A March 1944 report by the RAF's Air Fighting Development Unit made brief comparisons between the Mustang III (P-51B-1) and the Fw 190A powered by the BMW 801D. It stated that the latter was almost 50mph slower at all heights, increasing to 70mph above 28,000ft.

There appeared to be little to choose in the maximum rate of climb. It was anticipated that the Mustang III would have a better maximum climb than the Fw 190. The Mustang was considerably faster at all heights in a zoom climb, and it could always out-dive the Fw 190. When it came to the turning circle, the report stated that there was not much to choose. The Mustang was 'slightly better when evading an enemy aircraft with a steep turn. The pilot will always out-turn the attacking aircraft initially because of the difference in speeds. It is therefore still a worthwhile maneuver with the Mustang III when attacked.'

When it came to rate of roll, not even a Mustang III could rival the Fw 190A. The report concluded that;

In the attack, a high speed should be maintained or regained in order to regain height initiative. An Fw 190 could not evade by diving alone. In defense, a steep turn followed by a full throttle dive should increase the range before regaining height and course. Dogfighting is not altogether recommended. Do not attempt to climb away without at least 250 mph showing initially.

P-51 MUSTANG AND FW 190A COMPARISON SPECIFICATIONS

	P-51B/C	P-51D/K	Fw 190A-8
Powerplant	1,380hp V-1650-7	1,490hp V-1650-7	1,700hp BMW 801D radial
Dimensions			
Span	37ft 0in	37ft 0in	34ft 5$\frac{1}{2}$in
Length	32ft 3in	32ft 3in	29ft 4$\frac{1}{4}$in
Height	12ft 2in	12ft 2in	13ft 0in
Wing area	235.7sq ft	235.7sq ft	196.5sq ft
Weights			
Empty	6,985lb	7,125lb	7,680lb
Loaded	11,800lb	11,600lb	9,680lb
Performance			
Max speed	440mph at 30,000ft	437mph at 25,000ft	402mph at 20,700ft
Range	400 miles	950 miles	658 miles
Climb	to 20,000ft/7 min	to 3,475ft/1 min	to 26,300ft/14.4 min
Service Ceiling	41,800ft	41,900ft	32,700ft
Armament	4 x 0.50in Brownings	6 x 0.50in Brownings	4 x MG 151 20mm cannon 2 x MG 12.7mm machine guns

In his "Briefing for P-51 Pilot Instructors" in August 1945, Louis S. Wait, Administrative Test Pilot for North American Aviation at Inglewood, California, said, in part;

The new, heavier, more powerful Packard-built Rolls-Royce engine made necessary a heavier radiator for proper cooling and a heavier four-blade wide-chord propeller to utilize the increased engine power at altitude. The P-51B/C was an overloaded aeroplane since the combat weight was increased from 8,000lb to slightly over 9,000lb. As later results demonstrated, the decrease in "g" factor alone was not a serious complication. However, the increased engine power and four-blade propeller caused a marked decrease in directional stability.

Whereas the pilot previously had to use increasing rudder pressure for increasing sideslip or yaw angles, the rudder forces now tended to decrease at yaw angles greater than 100 degrees. If the pilot did not apply sufficient opposite rudder, the aeroplane tended to increase the skid or sideslip all by itself, eventually resulting in an unintentional snap roll or entry into a spin. Several pilots complained that they could no longer obtain their usual evasive action because of the addition of the dorsal fin and change in the rudder boost tab.

With full fuselage tanks and two 110-gallon external tanks, the gross weight of the P-51D was over 11,600lb, nearly 50 percent more than the design weight of the aeroplane. The only way to obtain increased strength or any substantial amount of increased stability would be to start from scratch and design a new aeroplane.

THE STRATEGIC SITUATION

After the war, the USAAF's ranking officer, Gen H H "Hap" Arnold, frankly admitted that it had been "the Army Air Force's own fault" that the Mustang had not been employed operationally very much earlier. Range was not something that had influenced the equipment of fighter units destined for the ETO because it was thought that operations would be similar to those undertaken by RAF fighters, where high-altitude performance seemed to be the important factor.

The Eighth Air Force had begun the bomber offensive from East Anglia in 1942 with the steadfast belief that tight bomber formations could fight their way unescorted to a target in the face of fighter opposition and still strike with acceptable losses.

The futility of the US tactics was finally rammed home during the bloody aerial battles fought in the autumn of 1943, when unescorted bombers penetrated deeper into Reich airspace than ever before and more than 60 "heavies" were lost on a single

Fw 190A-8/R2s of IV.(Sturm)/ JG 3 prepare to take off from Schöngau in August 1944, the unit being led aloft by Gruppenkommandeur Hauptmann Wilhelm Moritz. (Courtesy of Eddie Creek)

mission. Almost too late, the American chiefs of staff were immediately struck by the need to drastically overhaul the USAAF's long-range fighter cover.

At the same time, the massed raids by B-24s and B-17s on targets in Germany had sent shock waves through the Luftwaffe high command. The situation that confronted the Jagdwaffe in 1943 resulted in an urgent need for a fighter capable of breaking up the American combat box formations so that pilots could then pick off single bombers without fear of having to face the potentially destructive firepower that a mass formation could bring to bear. With the Fw 190 in the forefront of the defense of the Reich, the heavy bomber losses reached 18.2 percent in late 1943. A year earlier, when German targets had been defended predominantly by Bf 109Gs, the average American losses were 13.6 percent of the attacking force. In September–October 1943, almost a thousand Fw 190s were operating with units in France and Germany, and a further 270 were serving on the eastern front and in Italy.

After Schweinfurt, desperate attempts were made by the USAAF to improve fighter cover. The P-38 Lightning had a good escort range, but it was usually second best in combat with the Bf 109G and Fw 190A. Single-engined fighters such as the nimble Spitfire IX and P-47D Thunderbolt (an aircraft double the weight of a Bf 109 and half as much again as the Fw 190) had only enough range to escort the bombers part of the way and then meet them on their return. Eighth Air Force commander Gen Ira Eaker knew that deep penetration missions were finished unless a proven long-range escort fighter could be found. "At this point nothing was more critical than the early

Capt Don Gentile of the Debden-based 336th FS/ 4th FG watches his crew chief, Sgt John Ferra, update his victory tally beneath the cockpit of P-51B-7 43-6913 *Shangri-La*. Gentile claimed 21.833 aerial and six strafing kills flying Spitfire VBs, P-47C/Ds and P-51Bs in the ETO between August 1942 and April 1944. No fewer than 13 of these victories were against Fw 190s, including a trio of Focke-Wulf fighters knocked down near Ruhrburg on the afternoon of April 8, 1944. (USAF)

arrival of the P-38s and P-51s", he stated postwar. The P-51B was not only capable of meeting the Bf 109s and Fw 190s on even or better terms, it could also escort the B-24s and B-17s all the way to their targets and back home again.

The Mustang's range of 2,080 miles was far in excess of that available in other fighters of the day, and this was achieved through the combination of internal fuel tanks and external drop tanks. A total of 92 gallons were contained in fuel cells in each wing, and this was supplemented by two 75-gallon underwing drop tanks and an 85-gallon fuselage-mounted tank fitted as an afterthought behind the cockpit. When the latter was anything more than two-thirds full, the Mustang was afflicted by a potentially vicious handling peculiarity that meant that pilots could not perform even modest combat maneuvers. This left the fighter vulnerable, as even an average German fighter pilot could easily outmaneuver a Mustang that had a full fuselage tank. If such an attack occurred, the P-51 pilot would usually lose control due to the fighter's aft-loaded centre of gravity, pitching over and entering a fatal spin.

It was not long after Mustang pilots started flying long range missions into occupied Europe that reports began filtering back from the frontline concerning the fighter's handling when fueled up. With the full 85 gallons in the fuselage tank, the aft centre of gravity in a maximum-rate turn caused a stick reversal – the aeroplane tended to wrap the turn tighter without any backpressure on the stick. Pilots were quoted as stating that the P-51 "behaved like a pregnant sow."

The standard procedure was to burn the fuselage tank down to about 30 gallons immediately after take-off, and prior to switching to external tanks. That way if the

VIII Fighter Command's fighter groups were based in East Anglia so as to be as close to targets in occupied Europe as possible. Most of these airfields were built from scratch specially for the USAAF in a massive construction program launched in 1942.

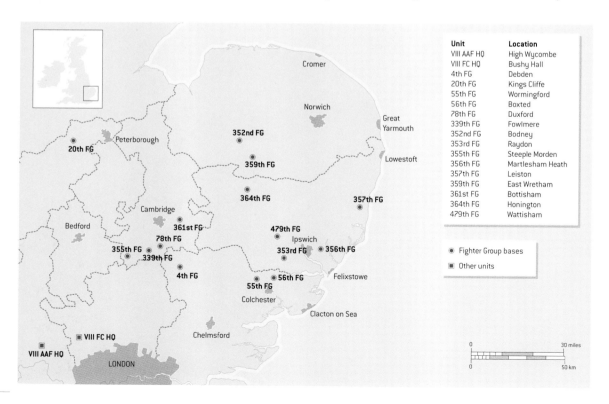

Unit	Location
VIII AAF HQ	High Wycombe
VIII FC HQ	Bushy Hall
4th FG	Debden
20th FG	Kings Cliffe
55th FG	Wormingford
56th FG	Boxted
78th FG	Duxford
339th FG	Fowlmere
352nd FG	Bodney
353rd FG	Raydon
355th FG	Steeple Morden
356th FG	Martlesham Heath
357th FG	Leiston
359th FG	East Wretham
361st FG	Bottisham
364th FG	Honington
479th FG	Wattisham

● Fighter Group bases
■ Other units

latter had to be jettisoned unexpectedly, the P-51 pilot was already in a condition from which he could fight. Theoretically, pilots would be well inside Germany before they exhausted their external fuel load, and the longer they could retain their external tanks the better.

The fuel-tank selector, which had five positions corresponding to the five tanks, controlled fuel flow. The selector was in the center of the cockpit below the instrument panel and just forward of the control column. Pilots would take off using fuel from the left side 75 gallon wing tank, and once airborne and in formation, they would switch to the fuselage tank situated aft of the cockpit. If the fuel selector was on one of the External positions when the tanks were dropped, the engine would start to run roughly as it sucked air, rather than fuel. No permanent harm was done, but the momentary silence of the Merlin in the cockpit invariably rattled the nerves of an already fraught new pilot – veterans also reported that it scared them too!

Although the Mustang would eventually be the straw that would break the back of the Jagdgruppen, from late 1943 until the early spring of 1944, the daylight bomber crews were, for the most part, still very much on their own against the Luftwaffe. Inexplicably, USAAF planners considered the P-51B better suited to tactical operations rather than strategic long-range bomber escort, and therefore in November 1943 the first deliveries of Merlin-powered Mustangs were made to three groups of the tactical Ninth Air Force in the UK, instead of the Eighth Air Force's VII Fighter Command, whose need was critical.

However, by the time the Ninth Air Force's first Mustang-equipped group (the 354th FG, aptly dubbed the "Mustang Pioneer Group") arrived in England in November 1943, Gen "Hap" Arnold had worked out a plan that would see P-51Bs escorting his clearly vulnerable heavy bombers before the year was out. Although the

As this map clearly shows, the Merlin-engined Mustang possessed an awesome range for a piston-engined fighter.

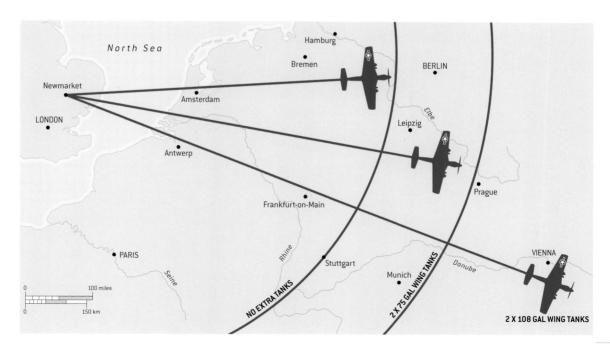

Capt Henry W. Brown was the top air and ground-strafing ace of the 355th FG, claiming 14.2 aerial and 14.5 strafing kills. He scored all of his victories whilst at the controls of a Mustang, including a pair of Fw 190s shot down in a P-51B and two more in a D-model. (Courtesy of William Hess)

354th FG was assigned to the Ninth Air Force for administration, operationally it would be controlled by the Eighth Air Force's VIII Fighter Command. Once in the UK, the "Mustang Pioneer Group" would have just two weeks to get itself ready for combat operations.

The unit flew its first operational mission over enemy territory from Boxted, on the Essex/Suffolk border, on December 1, and four days later it helped provide bomber escort for 452 B-17s and 96 B-24s sent to attack targets in the French city of Amiens – 34 P-38s and 266 P-47s also participated in this mission. On the 13th, when a record 649 bombers struck naval targets in Bremen, Hamburg and Kiel, P-51Bs reached the limit of their escort range for the first time.

On February 10, 1944, some 40 long-ranging P-51s accompanied the "heavies" to their targets and back again, but they were powerless to prevent a much larger force of German fighters destroying 29 of the 169 Flying Fortresses despatched. The very next day the first P-51Bs to be permanently assigned to VIII Fighter Command became operational with the 357th FG at Raydon, in Essex.

During "Big Week" (February 20–25), Eighth and Fifteenth Air Force bombers (the latter flying from bases in Italy) and 1,000 fighters were despatched almost daily on the deepest penetrations into Germany thus far. On March, 6 730 B-17s and B-24s and 801 P-38, P-47 and P-51 escort fighters headed for targets in the suburbs of Berlin in the first American air raid on "Big-B," as the German capital was nicknamed by USAAF crews. Eleven fighters and 69 bombers were lost, with a further 102 "heavies" seriously damaged.

"Big Week" and the early attacks on Berlin, provided the heyday for the P-47 Thunderbolt in its role as a bomber escort with VIII Fighter Command. Thereafter, the Luftwaffe would be opposed primarily by Mustangs, as its fighters vainly attempted to blunt the daylight bombing campaign. By war's end only one of VIII Fighter Command's fifteen fighter groups was not equipped with the P-51D/K, the Mustang's advantage of greater endurance over the P-47 having seen the aircraft wreak havoc throughout occupied Europe whilst escorting bombers on long-penetration raids deep into Germany and beyond.

Recently adorned with D-Day stripes, P-51Bs of the 361st FG's 376th FS taxi out at the start of a mission from Bottisham in early June 1944. All of these aircraft are equipped with a single metal 62 Imperial gallon auxiliary tank beneath each wing. (Courtesy of Steve Gotts)

D-DAY NUMBERS

On June 6, 1944, when the Allies stormed the beaches of Normandy, the Fw 190 fighter force, like the rest of the Luftwaffe in western France, offered little in the way of resistance when faced with overwhelming RAF and USAAF air power. More than 4,100 Allied fighters were committed in support of the D-Day landings, with some 2,300 of these being USAAF day fighters. In response, the Luftwaffe had just 425 fighters of all types in the area, of which only 250–280 were serviceable on any given day. Nevertheless, on occasion German fighters inflicted significant losses on the massed ranks of USAAF bombers and their escorts, but replacement aircrew and aircraft were rapidly drafted in and the offensive never wavered.

Mud-spattered Fw 190A-7 "Black 3" (Wk-Nr. 430352) of 2./JG 1 was photographed at Dortmund in January 1944. The 'winged 1' painted on the fighter's engine cowling had become the official emblem of JG 1 following the death in action of its *Kommodore*, 206-victory ace Major Hans Philipp, on October 8, 1943. (Seebrandt courtesy of Rob de Visser)

By early July the Allies had firmly established themselves in France, and VIII Fighter Command returned to its primary mission of heavy bomber support as the Eighth Air Force once again shifted its focus back to daylight raids on strategic targets. The Mustang pilots, dubbed "Little Friends" by the USAAF bomber crews, soon added ground strafing to their close escort and dogfighting repertoire as airfields and communications targets were battered by rockets, machine guns and bombs once the Allies gained the initiative in the skies over Germany.

The Luftwaffe, however, was still far from defeated, and production of fighter aircraft actually increased in 1944 and into 1945. It peaked in September 1944, when an astonishing 1874 Bf 109s and 1002 Fw 190s were completed. That same month, an average of three German fighters and two pilots were killed in action for every B-17 or B-24 shot down. The US Strategic Air Forces were clearly winning the war of attrition in the conflict with the Jagdwaffe, which was forced on the defensive. Irreparable harm was now being inflicted on the German fighter force through shortages of pilots, aircraft and fuel – problems that never afflicted American fighter groups.

January 1945 marked the Eighth Air Force's third year of operations, and it seemed as if the end of the war in Europe was now in sight. The Wehrmacht's December 1944 offensive in the Ardennes had ultimately petered out due to superior Allied air power, and in the east, the Red Army was in the early stages of its final push towards Germany.

Although an Allied victory was no longer in doubt, the last months of the war saw the surviving elements of the German armed forces put up a dogged defense of their homeland. And the dispersed manufacturing plants established throughout the Third Reich proved very difficult for the Eighth Air Force to neutralize, despite heavy bombers continuing to strike at these targets well into April 1945. And while the "heavies" sortied into enemy territory on a near-daily basis, so the Mustang escorts continued to offer them protection against the final remnants of the once mighty Luftwaffe in its final death throes.

THE COMBATANTS

The Fw 190A and the Merlin-engined Mustang were two of the truly great aircraft of World War II, the exploits of those that flew them ranking both types amongst the finest fighters in the annals of military aviation. Each possessed their own intrinsic and distinctive merits and, as with all fighters, they also had their shortcomings. But in the right hands these limitations could usually be compensated for.

Almost all the top American aces in the ETO flew the Mustang, and many of the leading German *experten* claimed their victories in the Fw 190A. When pitched against each other, combat experience, or the lack of it, was often the deciding factor. It must be remembered that by 1943–44, American Mustang pilots confronted scores of German fighter pilots that had been in continuous action in Europe since 1940. Apart from a few who had flown with the RAF in Spitfire-equipped "Eagle" squadrons, USAAF pilots arriving in the ETO from 1942 onwards were relatively new to their trade, and were not combat experienced. Most of their German opponents, by contrast, had already seen several years of aerial combat either on the Channel front or in the east against the USSR.

Luftwaffe pilot training could trace its lineage back to the late 1920s, when many future military aviators were trained to fly gliders due to the outlawing of an official German air arm by the Treaty of Versailles, signed in the aftermath of World War I. Then, in 1933, Adolf Hitler came to power and World War I ace Hermann Göring was appointed Germany's first Air Minister. Rearmament gathered pace, and on March 1, 1935 Nazi Germany revealed the Luftwaffe to the world. It comprised 20,000 men, many of whom had received flying training either as co-pilots with Lufthansa or in schools secretly set up for the purpose in the USSR.

An opportunity to try out Luftwaffe tactics and aircraft came in 1936 when the Spanish Civil War between General Franco's Nationalist forces and the Republicans

began. Hitler supported the Nationalists, and his pilots and crews in the Condor Legion learned many invaluable lessons which determined Luftwaffe fighter tactics in World War II.

AMERICAN PILOT TRAINING

Whilst the future cream of the Jagdwaffe's fighter force was receiving a blooding in the skies over Spain, across the Atlantic in the USA, the USAAC had finally recognized that it would face monumental problems in developing a tremendously expanded air arm should the war that now seemed inevitable in Europe escalate into a worldwide conflict. In early 1939, USAAC chief of staff Gen "Hap" Arnold realised that US military forces had to plan for the possibility of involvement in the European war. He and other senior officers in the USAAC duly devised a scheme that would facilitate the training of 1,200 pilots by the end of 1939, increasing to 7,000 in 1940 and a staggering 30,000 in 1941.

One of the Luftwaffe's most successful aces in the West, Hauptmann Hans Ehlers had claimed 55 victories by the time he was killed in combat with Mustangs from the 364th FG on 27 December 1944 – five other Fw 190 pilots died in the same engagement. A veteran of the battles of France and Britain, and *Gruppenkommandeur* of I./JG 1 at the time of his death, Ehlers had served with this unit since 3./JG 3 had been redesignated 6./JG 1 in January 1942. Included in his victory tally were no fewer than 24 four-engined bombers and four P-51s. (Courtesy of Eddie Creek)

The USAAC could not accomplish this task alone, however, so Arnold's scheme called for the establishment of civilian-operated training schools. The latter would be responsible for the primary training phase of flight instruction, with civilian schools providing all services and facilities, bar the aircraft, but with USAAC control of the methods and manner of the instruction. In the spring of 1939 eight successful civilian pilot training school owner-operators agreed to become contractors with the USAAC to provide primary pilot training for 12,000 pilots per month. The program that Arnold recommended was to take up to 36 weeks to complete, with 12 weeks each for primary, basic and advanced pilot training (ultimately, the USAAC decided that these training sessions would be conducted in ten-week periods so as to save time).

By July 1939 nine civilian schools were giving primary phase flying training to USAAC Aviation Cadets. Within 12 months nine more schools were in operation, and by the end of 1940, Arnold's ambitious expansion program would be training more than 30,000 pilots a year. One such school was Darr Aero Tech, located four miles southwest of Albany, New York, which by September 14, 1940 had its first class of 50 American cadets conducting training flights with its 15 USAAC-supplied

Mustangs, Thunderbolts and a solitary Lightning come together at Bottisham, in Cambridgeshire, on August 31, 1944 for an VIII Fighter Command group COs' conference. P-51D *GENTLE ANNIE* was flown in by Col Harold Rau, CO of the 20th FG, while 44-14111 *Straw Boss 2* was the mount of Lt Col James Mayden, CO of the 352nd FG. P-47D-25 42-26641 *Hairless Joe* was assigned to Col Dave C Schilling, CO of the 56th FG, P-51D 44-14291 *DA QUAKE* was 55th FG CO Col John L "Jarring John" McGlinn's machine, and P-47D *Judy* was flown by Col Phil Tukey, CO of the 356th FG. The natural metal P-47D was assigned to Col Ben Rimmerman, CO of the 353rd FG, and the P-38J at right was 479th FG Col "Hub" Zemke's machine. Finally, the checker-nosed P-47D partially visible alongside the Lightning was the aircraft of 78th FG CO Col Frederic Gray. (USAF)

Stearmans. One of the first to graduate from the school as part of Class 41J was future ranking Mustang ace George E Preddy, who had actually flown 300 hours prior to enlisting.

By early 1942 the bulk of the US training program was being carried out by the Technical Training Command and Flying Training Command (renamed USAAF Training Command in 1943). By 1944, the standard USAAC program for the minimum number of hours required to produce a qualified pilot was 65 hours in Primary training, 70 in Basic training and 75 in Advanced training. Primary training consisted of 225 hours of ground school instruction and 65 hours of flight training to produce cadets who could fly single-engined, elementary aircraft. Most recruits had never even driven a car before, let alone flown an aircraft, but they were expected to fly solo after just six hours of tuition.

Potential pilots who reached the Primary stage arrived via Classification and Pre-Flight Training. College Training Detachments were also established by the USAAF in early 1943, and everyone entering the Aviation Cadet Program from then until the end of the war was assigned to one of these detachments for a period of between one and five months, depending on the scores the recruits had achieved during a battery of tests administered during Basic Training and at the College Training Detachment.

By 1942 the USAAF had four Classification and Pre-Flight Centers in Nashville, Tennessee, Maxwell Field, Alabama, San Antonio, Texas, and Santa Ana, California. Classification consisted of general education tests, with 50 questions per test in multiple-choice form, physiomotor tests (to test coordination) and a 64-point physical examination. Those who did not 'wash out' awaited cadet classification for pilot pre-flight training. The latter normally lasted from seven to ten weeks, during which time cadets attended academic classes, marched in formation, took part in PT and drill, learned to fire a pistol and undertook aquatic training, where they learned ditching procedures. Cadet pilots studied armaments and gunnery, with 30 hours spent on sea and air recognition, 48 hours on codes, 24 hours on physics, 20 hours on mathematics and 18 hours on maps and charts. All who were successful moved on to the next stage of flight training. Potential pilots were now given the chance to learn to fly.

An average of 600 potential pilots attended each Primary training school, students spending 94 hours on academic work in ground school, 54 hours on military training and 60 hours in 125–225hp PT-13/17 or PT-21/22 open-cockpit biplanes or PT-19/23/26 low-wing monoplanes.

The standard Primary school flight training was divided into four phases. The first was the pre-solo phase, which saw students taught the general operation of a light aircraft, proficiency in landing techniques and recovery from stalls and spins.

The second phase covered a pre-solo work review and development of precision control by flying patterns such as elementary "figure 8s", "lazy 8s", "pylon 8s" and "chandelles." In the third phase, students developed a high proficiency in "shooting approaches" and actual landings. Finally, the fourth phase focused exclusively on aerobatics.

During this training, at least half of the flights would be made with an instructor and the remainder would see the pilot flying solo. Each cadet had to make at least 175 landings. Those who soloed went on to basic flying training school, where they undertook a ten-week course. Here, a further 70 hours was flown in a 450hp BT-13/15 basic trainer (later replaced by the AT-6, because the BT was considered to be too easy to fly), 94 hours spent in ground school and 47 hours conducting military training.

Three P-51D-5s of the 335th FS and a solitary machine from the 336th FS form up for the camera in August 1944. Leading the formation is 4th FG CO, and 14.5-kill ace, Col Don Blakeslee, and his wingman in 'WD-A' is Capt Bob Church. A legendary figure in VIII Fighter Command, Blakeslee led the first Merlin Mustang missions in the ETO. He claimed 6.5 Fw 190s destroyed, 2.5 of these whilst flying the P-51. (USAF)

In ground school, five major topics were covered; aircraft and equipment (understanding the aircraft and how everything worked, including engines and mechanical theory); navigation (preparation for cross-country flights); aircraft recognition (both 'friendly' and hostile); principles of flight; and, finally, radio codes and radio communication for pilots. A link trainer was also available for use by rated pilots, and this introduced cadets to the art of instrument flying.

By the end of basic school, trainees would have learned to fly an aircraft competently. Further training taught them to pilot a warplane the USAAF way. Before the end of basic training, trainees were classified – on the basis of choice and instructors' reports – for single-engine training (fighter pilots) or twin-engine training (bomber, transport or twin-engined fighter pilots). There were two final stages in the training phase prior to a pilot reaching the frontline – advanced flying training and transition flying training. Advanced flying training was a ten-week course (single-engine and twin engine), involving 70 hours flying, 60 hours ground school and 19 hours military training. Single-engine trainees flew 600hp AT-6s during this period, and also used the aircraft to undertake a course in fixed gunnery.

At the end of advanced training the graduates were awarded the silver pilot's wings of the USAAF and appointed flight officers or commissioned as second lieutenants. Transition flying training followed, pilots learning to fly the type of aircraft they would

The 357th FG's top four aces are seen together at the group's Yoxford base during the autumn of 1944. Between them they claimed 67.75 aerial victories. Capt Bud Peterson (left) was credited with 15.5 kills, including 5.5 Fw 190s, Maj Kit Carson bagged 18.5, with 11 Fw 190s destroyed, Maj Johnny England got 16.5, including five Fw 190s, and Capt Bud Anderson (right) 16.25, with nine Fw 190s shot down. (Courtesy of Merle C Olmsted)

take into combat. Fighter pilots received a five-week transition course, with single-engine pilots flying ten hours in aircraft like the P-39, P-40, P-47 or P-51. Gunnery was part of fighter transition training.

At the conclusion of transition training, pilots reported to unit training groups, where they were welded into fighting teams. Between December 1942 and August 1945, 35,000 day-fighter crews were trained. All fighter units were supplied by the operational training unit program. Simultaneously, a replacement unit training program (90-day course) within the four domestic air forces provided replacements for overseas aircrew who had been lost in combat or rotated home for reassignment.

The USAAF's School of Applied Tactics (AAFSAT) in Orlando, Florida, was established on October 9, 1942 for the purpose of training selected officers under simulated combat conditions. The number of graduates between November 1942 and VJ-Day totaled almost 54,000 (two-thirds of them were USAAF personnel). A system of 12 airfields – ranging from a vacant field to a large bomber base with 10,000ft runways dotted around in a "war theater" of 8,000 square miles – was created to allow the mounting of war games involving 'enemy' bombers and fighters. The mission of AAFSAT was to train USAAF cadres (the personnel framework around which all new combat groups were formed), to test and develop new techniques, and to accelerate the spread of new developments and methods to the theaters of combat.

Six months was initially required after the formation of a cadre to complete the organization and training of a new group. By 1943, preparations to move an air unit overseas had been cut to just over four months. It normally took almost 120 days and 17 separate actions by HQ officers just to move the unit to its port of embarkation.

GERMAN PILOT TRAINING

In Germany, pilot recruitment and training was strongly influenced by Prussian military tradition. Prewar, and up to the end of 1940, all future officers and NCOs alike could expect to undertake six months of basic infantry training at a *Flieger-Ersatzabteilung*. Following the completion of this induction period, all recruits were reviewed for possible advancement as possible pilots. Likely candidates were sent to a *Flug-Anwärterkompanie* (aircrew candidate company) for evaluation in a series of tests in basic aviation theory.

With the growing demand for pilots following the commencement of World War II, the Luftwaffe's training and recruiting staff rationalized and compressed the initial stages of aircrew selection to enable trainees to embark upon the most appropriate training regime more expeditiously. The *Flieger-Ersatzabteilung* was now replaced by a series of *Flieger-Ausbildungsregiments*, where recruits would receive basic military training and preliminary aviation instruction. Potential pilots were then sent to undergo the standard selection process within a *Flug-Anwärterkompanie*, where the rest of their basic training, conducted over a period of three to four months, was completed alongside the aircrew evaluation tests.

Upon assignment to a *Flug-Anwärterkompanie*, the *Flugzeugführer-Anwärter* (pilot candidate) would receive instruction in basic flight theory and rudimentary aeronautics in aircraft such as the Bü 131, Ar 66C, He 72 Kadet, Go 145 and Fw 44 Stieglitz biplane trainers. Assessed for advancement throughout this phase, candidates displaying the required aptitude were then sent to *Flugzeugführerschule A/B* as soon as a space became available – typically two months after arriving at the *lug-Anwärterkompanie*. Here, flight training proper would be undertaken.

At such schools, students underwent four principal levels of instruction, each requiring qualification for its own license, before advancing to the next stage. These licenses, earned over a period of six to nine months, gave the schools their name. The *A1-Schien* introduced students to basic practical flying in dual-controlled training aircraft, instructors teaching recruits how to take-off and land, recover from stalls and attain their solo flight rating. In the early stages of the war, instructors would have been assigned four trainees each, but by 1942 this number had risen to six.

At the *A2-Schien*, cadets were required to learn the theory of flight, including aerodynamics, meteorology, flying procedures and aviation law, as well as the practical application of aeronautical engineering, elementary navigation, wireless procedure and Morse code. In the air, they gained more flying experience on larger single-engine aircraft.

The next level of training, known as the *B1-Schien*, saw pilots progress onto high-performance single- and twin-engined machines typically fitted with a retractable undercarriage – if destined to fly fighters, older types of combat aircraft such as early

Pilots from II./JG 26 walk out to their Fw 190A-6s at Cambrai-Epinoy in February 1944. Third from left is Oberfeldwebel 'Addi' Glunz, then *Staffelkapitän* of 5./JG 26. He was one of the most successful German fighter pilots in the west in early 1944, and survived the war with 71 kills (including 19 heavy bombers) to his credit. (Courtesy of Eddie Creek)

Bf 109s would be flown for the first time. Students would then undertake training aimed at acquiring the final *B2-Schien*, having accumulated 100 to 150 hours of flight time over the previous 14 to 17 months – this figure had been cut to just 40 hours in a matter of weeks by war's end.

In late 1940 the *Flugzeugführerschule A/B* was streamlined to take into account wartime demand for pilots, with a far greater emphasis now being placed on practical flying skills from the outset. The A2 license was dropped, with that phase being amalgamated into the remaining grades.

The A-license generally took three months to complete, with the B phase seeing pilots flying more advanced types. An elementary *K1 Kunstflug* (stunt-flying) aerobatics course was also included in the latter phase to provide all pilots with a good understanding of rudimentary evasive maneuvers (barrel rolls, loops and formation splits). This phase also allowed instructors to identify any potential fighter pilots among their students, who thereafter received extra flying time.

Upon completion of the B2 phase, the cadet would finally be granted his *Luftwaffeflugzeugführerschein* (air force pilots' license), accompanied by the highly prized *Flugzeugführerabzeichen* (pilot's badge) – his "wings". After an average of ten to 13 months at *Flugzeugführerschule A/B*, he was now a fully qualified pilot.

It was at this point that new pilots were categorized for service on single- or multi-engined aircraft, with each being assigned to a specialist flying school. Here, he would undergo intensive training for his allotted aircraft type, with potential fighter pilots being sent directly to *Jagdfliegervorschulen* or *Waffenschule* for three to four months, where they carried out 50 hours of flying on semi-obsolescent types. For Fw 190 pilots in 1943–44, this usually meant Ar 68 and He 51 biplanes (becoming progressively rare by then), Bf 109D/Es, captured French Dewoitine D.520s and Ar 96s. By the time he was eventually posted to a frontline unit, a pilot could expect to have 200 hours of flying time under his belt.

The Luftwaffe's usual training of pilots for Defence of the Reich duties was at times rudimentary in the extreme. Here, a white-capped *oberleutnant* uses models to demonstrate a frontal attack on a trio of B-17s. (Courtesy of John Weal)

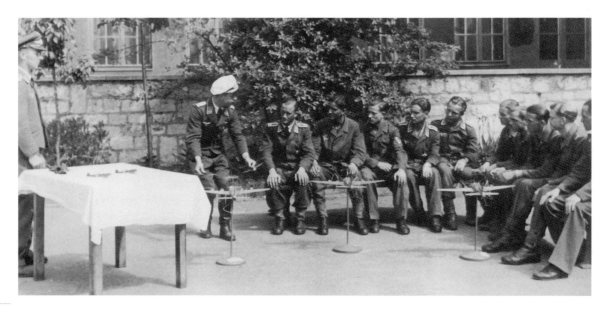

The realities of war led the Luftwaffe to further modify the final stages of its training syllabus in 1940, with the creation of Erganzungsgruppen (Operational Training Schools) for the teaching of tactics and further familiarization with frontline types. In the Jagdwaffe, these units were directly linked, and controlled, by operational *geschwader*. Designated IV. *Gruppe*, the intention of these units was to allow new pilots to gain precious operational experience before ultimately being hurled into combat against the enemy.

By the summer of 1942, the loss of so many experienced pilots meant that there was insufficient manpower available to carry out the training function in operational squadrons, and this became more and more abbreviated. Erganzungsgruppen attached to frontline fighter units were therefore disbanded in mid 1942 and replaced by three Fighter Pools located in the three main operational areas for the Luftwaffe – in the South at Cazeaux, in France (ErganzungsJagdgruppe Süd), in the West at Mannheim, in Germany (ErganzungsJagdgruppe West), and in East at Krakow, in Poland (ErganzungsJagdgruppe Ost).

All operational units would draw replacement crews from these pools until war's end. Although the creation of these pools reduced the number of instructors required, thus freeing up more experienced pilots for combat, it also effectively curtailed the operational training of new pilots in the frontline just at the time when such experience was critically needed for newcomers receiving their first exposure to action. Just as serious was the elimination of a fully-crewed, but only partially trained, reserve that the Erganzungsgruppen offered to frontline units.

For those pilots destined to fly the Fw 190 in 1943–45, the trio of ErganzungsJagdgruppen were equipped with a varied fleet of Focke-Wulf fighters covering all major variants. There were also a handful of two-seat Fw 190S-5/8s (S standing for *Schule*) on strength, although these were vastly outnumbered by conventional single-seaters.

Fw 190A-7 Wk-Nr. 340283 "Yellow 6" of 3./JG 1 is refueled by ground personnel at Dortmund in January 1944. This aircraft was lost in combat with American heavy bombers on February 8, 1944, Feldwebel Gerhard Giese perishing when the aircraft crashed near Charleville. (Seebrandt courtesy of Rob de Visser)

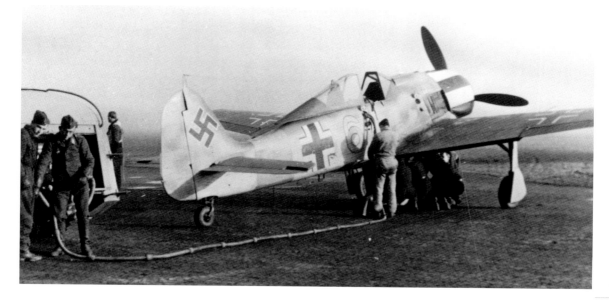

Staffelkapitän Oberleutnant Waldemar "Waldi" Radener leads 7./JG 26 in his Fw 190A-8 "Brown 4" Wk.-Nr. 340001 on a patrol from Coesfeld-Stevede on May 4, 1944. Note the 20 victory bars on the rudder of Radener's aircraft. Exactly one week after this photograph was taken, Radener accidentally rammed a Liberator over France in Fw 190A-8 "Brown 2" and was forced to bail out with minor injuries. He survived the war with 37 victories to his credit, this tally including 12 heavy bombers, 11 P-47s, five Spitfires and two P-51s. (Courtesy of Eddie Creek)

Between January and April 1944, the Luftwaffe's day-fighter arm lost more than 1,000 aviators in action (many to P-51 pilots), which included the core of its experienced fighter leader cadre. One of the replacements drafted in to make good these losses was 21-year-old Helmut Peter Rix;

As soon as I was old enough I took up gliding, and with a C Class glider pilot's license, I joined the Luftwaffe on March 1, 1943. I had been accepted as an officer candidate and reported to Oschatz, in Saxony, for six weeks' basic training. From there we were posted to *Luftkriegsschule* (LKS) 3 at Werder/Havel, near Potsdam. Apart from more basic training, this was the stage at which serious officer training really commenced. Those with glider experience were placed in a special group, which worked up to the advanced glider pilot license using aircraft tow. Our powered flying then began with instruction on Bü 131 and Bü 181 primary trainers, and I eventually went solo on my 32nd circuit.

For the A2 license, we branched out into aerobatics and were introduced to long-distance flying. Parallel with our flying went instruction related to aircraft technical data, navigation and to becoming future officers.

Flying progression was subsequently made onto B2 training aircraft, bringing us into contact with W 33s and W 34s and twin-engined Caudron C 445s. These types were bigger and heavier, and this training phase included blind flying, formation flying, target landings and long distance triangular flights, with students alternating as first and second pilots. Nightflying, "circuits and bumps" and instrument flying was also included. My time at the officers' cadet school was hard in both the physical and mental sense, but it proved to be very rewarding. We were given our pilot's wings and I was promoted to fahnenjünker gefreiter.

Having been streamed for multi-engined nightfighters rather than day fighters, in early January 1944 I was posted to the B34 Blind Flying School at Kastrup, in Copenhagen. Here, I flew Ju 88A-4/5s, Ju 86s, He 111s, Siebel 204s and Ju 52/3ms. This was a very intensive program, with technical instruction on all the foregoing types, especially the Si 204 and Ju 88. Conversion went without a hitch and I was soon flying solo.

When our course ended in July 1944, we received our advanced pilot's wings, and as I waited to become a nightfighter pilot on Bf 110s and Me 410s, we were posted to Bad Aibling, in southern Germany. At the same time I was promoted to fahnenjünker-unteroffizier. Out of the blue came the announcement that our nightfighter training program had been cancelled, and we were given a choice of becoming single-seat all weather fighter pilots or going to the parachute regiment! For me the choice was easy – I wanted to fly, and with all the specialized training we had had, choosing the Fw 190 was obvious. Things then happened fast.

At the beginning of September 1944 I was posted to Jagdgeschwader 110 (part of ErganzungsJagdgruppe West) at Pretzsch, on the River Elbe, for conversion training. After flying heavy twins, it was quite something to sit in an advanced trainer like the single-engined Ar 96. The handling qualities were completely different to anything I had flown before – the effect was similar to having been driving a bus then being told to switch to a racing car. I soon settled in to enjoy the freedom and excitement of flying the Arado. Besides carrying on from where I had left off with instrument flying, I also got a taste of close formation flying in *Rotte* (two) and *Schwarm* (four) elements, nightflying and, for the first time, target practice.

On November 2, 1944 we moved to Altenburg for conversion onto the Fw 190. After three flights in a two-seat Fw 190S-8, I went solo while carrying out circuits – we were limited to five take-offs and landings each day under normal circumstances due to fuel shortages and Allied fighter activity. We continued fighter training over the firing range and made close formation flights in twos and fours at altitudes up to 30,000 ft. In mid-December we moved to Neustadt/Glewe to join 1 *Staffel* of the operational training unit I./JG 2 *ErganzungsGeschwader* for more intensive combat training, which took in high altitude flying with the entire *Staffel* and dogfighting. We did not stay long, and on January 12, 1945 I was posted to II./JG 301's 8 *Staffel* at Welzow.

My introduction to frontline flying was not good. My fellow pilots and I had hardly had time to get acquainted before the "scramble" order came through – eight out of ten of my new comrades did not return! Things were beginning to get very bad, with

Hauptmann Wilhelm Moritz sits on the cockpit sill of his Fw 190A-8/R2 (Wk-Nr. 681382) at Schöngau in August 1944. Like its 44-kill pilot, this IV.(Sturm)/JG 3 machine survived the war. (Courtesy of Eddie Creek)

Mustangs from the 487th FS/ 352nd FG soak up the sun at Bodney, in Norfolk, in the autumn of 1944. The unit introduced a 12-inch blue cowling band in early April 1944 as its group marking, and by month-end this had been extended aft to cover the black anti-dazzle panel too. (Courtesy of Bill Espie)

shortages of everything. We newly trained fighter pilots were supposed to gain some flying experience with the squadron before being sent into action, but that never materialized. Instead, we were just thrown straight into action.'

At 1015hrs on March 2, 1945, Helmut Peter Rix was scrambled in an Fw 190 from Stendal with other elements of JG 301 when Eighth Air Force heavy bombers and their escorts were detected heading for targets in Germany. He was part of a *Schwarm* led by Staffelkapitan Leutnant Walter Kropp, with the remaining aircraft being flown by Unteroffiziers H Hager and W Ehrlich. Rix recalled;

It was a beautiful morning, with clear blue sky, but with a cloud cover of 8/10ths at about 14,000ft. I climbed on a southeastly course to 24,000ft, where we spotted our target – a formation of B-17s at 27,000ft dead ahead. We were in line abreast formation and ready for a frontal attack when Kropp broke away to the left into a dive. Following our leader down, we got into a line astern formation – I was No 4.

At approximately 1100hrs, Rix's Fw 190 was destroyed by gunfire from P-51Ds flown by Capt Lee Kilgo and Lt Earl Mundell of the 486th FS/352nd FG, which was escorting B-17s of the 1st Force. All four Fw 190s were shot down during this battle, with Rix being the only one to survive.

COMBAT

MUSTANG TACTICS

When it came to implementing aerial tactics, the P-51's group leader was the "quarterback of the team". VIII Fighter Command units invariably employed the standard three-squadron formation when escorting bombers over occupied Europe, with each squadron composed of a quartet of four-ship flights and two aircraft as mission spares. The down-sun squadron flew 2,000–3,000ft above the lead unit, while the up-sun squadron positioned itself about 1,000ft below the lead unit. Each squadron flew about 3,000ft horizontally apart from the lead unit.

When it came to offensive tactics, 17.5-victory ace Capt John B England, CO of the 362nd FS/357th FG, opined that the most perfect bounce would be made from out of the sun, and from 3,000–5,000ft above the enemy;

A pilot making a bounce should always instinctively have the advantage in speed or altitude, since one can be converted into the other. Flights should fly close formation, relying on mutual support for protection. The enemy will think twice before he jumps 18 aeroplanes in good formation. This has been proven many times by our experience.

The best defensive maneuver for the P-51 against the common enemy fighter aeroplane is just a simple tight turn. I have never seen one of our fighters shot down in a tight turn, but I have seen our fighters shot down while trying to evade the enemy by diving to the deck, or pulling some fancy maneuvers. I say never be on the defensive list – if you are on the defensive, turn it into an offensive situation immediately. Always let the Hun know you're after him from the beginning.

Fellow ace Maj John A Storch (10.5 kills), who was CO of the 357th FG's 364th FS, related at the time;

The basic defensive maneuver is to turn into the attacking enemy. Often this will automatically turn a defensive situation into an offensive one. If the German turns with you, the P-51 should be on the tail of the average enemy aeroplane in short order. If, as we have found to be more often the case, the German split-esses for the deck, without top cover, you can split-ess after him. He may out dive you on the way down and out maneuver you during this dive, but when you level out on the deck you will probably be able to catch him.

When attacked by superior numbers, if no cloud cover or help is available, about the only thing you can do is to keep turning into his attacks and take such shots as you can get, hoping to even things up. You should, under such circumstances, continue to watch all the time for an opportunity to make a break for home. However, it does not pay to straighten out on a course unless you are very sure you will be out of accurate firing range. My own opinion is that the best way to make the break is a shallow dive with everything full forward. If the enemy starts to overhaul you again and gets within accurate range, about the only thing to do is to turn again and force him to take a deflection shot at you.

When attacked I like to have my wingman stay close enough that he can take an aeroplane off my tail, and I can do the same for him. He is of no help, however, if he stays in so tight that we cannot maneuver, and are practically one target. The preceding and following statements are completely dependent upon circumstances, and no hard and fast rules can be set down.

When attacking an enemy aircraft, the leader should go in for the first shot while his wingman drops out and back far enough that he can watch the sky and clear his own, and his leader's, tail. If the leader overshoots or has to break off his attack, his wingman

This quartet of Bottisham-based 374th FS/361st FG Mustangs was photographed from a 91st BG B-17G when returning from a bomber escort mission to Munich on July 11, 1944. The aircraft nearest to the camera is P-51B-15 42-106839 *BALD EAGLE III*, flown by 1Lt Robert T Eckfeldt. Next in line is P-51D-5 44-13357 B7-R *TIKA IV*, which was assigned to 1Lt Vernon Richards, then P-51D-5 44-13857 and Malcolm-hooded P-51B-15 42-106942. (Courtesy of Tom Cushing)

will be in position to start firing with the leader covering him. If you have to break off combat but want another shot later, break up and either turn to the right or left, but not in a turn of 360 degrees, as you probably will be unable to catch the enemy aircraft after you complete it.

Fw 190 TACTICS

Maj Storch also accurately described the tactics used by Fw 190s that he encountered over Germany in 1944–45;

The main enemy evasive tactics we have noticed are split-essing for the deck, going to cloud cover, rolling, sliding, slipping and bailing out. In any case, except for the last, the only thing to do is to follow him shooting, or if you think he will be unable to get away, wait until he straightens out and gives you a decent target. If the German has superior numbers in a large gaggle formation, you can usually get on a straggler or take on one of the aeroplanes towards the edges of the formation and try to separate him from the others. The others may not miss him.

If the enemy aircraft are flying in a gaggle-type formation, there isn't a lot they can do about it. Of course, you must have altitude on the German so you will have superior speed to break away should you get into trouble. Flaps can be used to avoid overshooting, but once you put them down you will have lost your speed advantage, and perhaps become vulnerable to attack. The best shooting method for us is get in as close as you can and still avoid hitting his aeroplane, or any pieces that by chance may fall off it, and let 'er rip. Anyone will do his best shooting when he is so close that he cannot miss.

These tactics took time to refine, and their success was ably demonstrated on several occasions. On April 8, 1944, for example, Mustangs in the 4th FG were one of the fighter groups that supported the bombers attacking Brunswick, and they attacked three separate gaggles of Fw 190s and Bf 109s over a 30-mile area from 23,000ft down to the deck. Altogether, the 4th FG claimed 33 fighters destroyed and nine damaged.

Three days later, when the 352nd FG provided penetration and withdrawal support for B-17s, the "Blue Nosed Bastards" (the group's P-51s were marked with blue noses as their identifying color) flew 40 minutes of escort before breaking away to strafe ground targets. They claimed three aerial victories and seven more aircraft destroyed on the ground.

Amongst those pilots to achieve success on this date was future 7.5-kill ace 1Lt Frank A. Cutler in P-51B-7 43-6578 *Soldier's Vote*. Spotting a locomotive just leaving the bridge across the Elbe River at Torgau, Cutler made his pass at the engine and saw pieces of it thrown up in the cloud of steam from its erupting boiler.

He then flew over the town of Torgau at rooftop height, heading west for a mile or two. Minutes later Cutler shared in the destruction of a lone Ju 52/3m, and as he headed north, watching the unfortunate transport aircraft go down, he spotted two light blue/gray Fw 190A-7s flying wingtip to wingtip directly below him in a westerly direction at about 1,000ft. Unteroffiziers Heinz Voigt and Karl Weiss of 4./JG 26 were flying the fighters on what should have been a routine transfer flight between bases. However, they happened to be in the wrong place at the wrong time. Cutler headed for them and closed fast, firing on the Fw 190 on the right from a distance of about 100 yards. His combat report stated;

1Lt Frank A. Cutler and his crew chief SSgt Cy Hall of the 486th FS/352nd FG are seen on the wing of P-51B-10 *GIG'S UP II* at Bodney. On 11 April 1944, Cutler, who was leading "Blue" Flight in P-51B-7 43-6578 *Soldier's Vote*, shot down a Ju 52/3m and two Fw 190A-7s from 4./JG 26 to take his score to 4.5 victories (the Ju 52/3m kill was reduced to a half-share upon Cutler's return to Bodney). Having "made ace" on May 8, 1944, Cutler was killed in a mid-air collision with a Bf 109G over Germany five days later. (Courtesy of Bill Espie)

JOHN C. MEYER

John C. Meyer was born on April 3, 1919 in Brooklyn, New York, and he subsequently attended Dartmouth College. He joined the Army Reserves and became a flying cadet, being commissioned a pilot and second lieutenant on July 26, 1940 at Kelly Field, in Texas. His first assignment was as a flight instructor, and he remained in this posting for a year. Meyer was then transferred to the 33rd Pursuit Squadron in Iceland to fly convoy patrols, before returning to the USA to join the 352nd FG in Massachusetts. He was made commanding officer of the group's 487th FS on December 28, 1942.

Meyer became a captain on January 21, 1943 and took the P-47-equipped 487th to Britain that June. The unit commenced combat operations in September, flying a series of bomber escort missions. On November 26, the now Maj Meyer scored his first victory when he downed a Bf 109. During April 1944 the unit began converting to the Mustang, and Meyer enjoyed his first success in the North American fighter on April 10, when he shared in the destruction of an Fw 190 and downed another Bf 109. On May 8, he celebrated his promotion to the rank of lieutenant colonel with a triple-kill haul that gave him ace status.

Meyer and the Mustang were a formidable duo, and he pushed his score past the 20-kill mark — this tally included two "triples" and a "double" haul, and he downed 8.5 Fw 190s in total. It is believed that Meyer claimed as many as 11.5 aerial kills in P-51D-15 44-15041 *Petie 3rd*. He is seen here sitting in that aircraft.

Perhaps Meyer's "finest hour" as CO of the 487th FS came in the battle now known as the legend of Y-29, when the "Bluenosers" destroyed 23 German fighters sent to attack the 352nd FG's Asch base, in Belgium, at dawn on January 1, 1945 as part of Operation *Bodenplatte*. The 487th FS was responsible for the bulk of these victories, earning the squadron the Distinguished Unit Citation — an honor usually reserved for groups. Meyer, who claimed two Fw 190s destroyed, was awarded his third DSC. This action cemented his reputation as one of the best fighter leaders in the ETO, as his long-time armorer Sgt Jim Bleidner recalled;

"While it is true that he showed extraordinary heroism on New Year's Day 1945, it is also true that his planning ahead and ability to think like a "German" played a very important role. In this case, he was convinced that the Germans would believe that the forward airfields would be vulnerable on New Year's Day because the pilots and crews would have large hangovers from the night before. Meyer called his pilots together on New Year's Eve and said no parties until the following night. As it happened, he was correct in his analysis."

On January 4,1945, Meyer's second combat tour in the ETO came to a premature end when the ammunition carrier he was traveling in as a passenger left a snow-covered road in Belgium and he suffered a serious leg injury. He was sent home to recuperate.

Staying in the air force postwar, Meyer served in Korea (with two MiG-15 kills to his name) and eventually rose to the rank of General. He retired in 1974 and died the following year. His final victory tally was 26 confirmed, one probable and three damaged, plus 13 strafing kills.

P-51B-7 43-6578 *Soldier's Vote* was used by future ace 1Lt Frank A Cutler on April 11, to destroy two Fw 190s and a Ju 52/3m. (Courtesy of Bill Espie)

I saw strikes on the tail section, so I skidded left and fired at the second aeroplane, which had not yet taken any evasive action. All my ammo was gone, but the pilot must have been hit since the Focke-Wulf whipped over to the left and exploded in the middle of the field. Then I noticed that the first Fw 190 was burning in the next field a few hundred yards away. I was separated from my flight and the Group, so I climbed to 23,000ft and came home alone.

Promoted to captain on May 2, 1944, Frank Cutler would subsequently lose his own life nine days later when his Mustang (P-51B-10 42-106483) collided with a Bf 109G south of Grimmen, in Germany.

ACES HIGH

On May 19, 1944, 1Lt Ray S Wetmore (who already had 4.25 kills to his name flying P-47Ds) of the 359th FG's 370th FS claimed the first of his 16 victories in Mustangs when he destroyed two Bf 109Gs. He downed two Fw 190s ten days later, and by war's end had increased his tally to 21.25 victories – 9.5 of these were Focke-Wulf fighters, including four destroyed and one shared destroyed on January 14, 1945.

The ranking ace of the 359th FG, Ray Wetmore's philosophy in combat was to close in to a distance where he still had a reasonable chance of being able to break off his attack without colliding with the enemy aircraft. He did not believe in head-on attacks, and would not break head-on into Fw 190s that boasted two 20mm cannon as part of their armament. He usually chose to break to one side of the Focke-Wulf and wait for his opponent's next move. Wetmore relied on the P-51's unmatched rate of turn, firmly believing that the Mustang was absolutely the best defensive weapon in the skies over Germany.

He also preferred the half roll to the split-ess. This was because during a half roll, the Mustang pilot could see the enemy much better than when performing a split-ess, and the American fighter did not gain too much speed during the maneuver. The P-51 was at its best when making a coordinated turn on the verge of stalling, regardless of its speed – Wetmore would consider a high-speed stall at any altitude above 500ft. He also said that German fighter pilots were at their most vulnerable when trying to take evasive action.

Yet despite the Mustang's superiority, well flown Fw 190As could still inflict losses on VIII Fighter Command. For example, on September 17, 1944, the 4th and 361st FGs were among those groups who tussled with JG 26 in the mid-afternoon. For four pilots killed in action, the jagdflieger claimed three Mustangs from the latter group and two from the 4th FG.

The 335th FS/4th FG had been bounced by 15 Fw 190A-8s from 8./JG 26 near Emmerich at the beginning of the engagement, and Leutnant Wilhelm Hofmann and Oberfahnrich Gerhard "Bubi" Schulwitz had shot down two of the P-51s. Moments later, 10.333-victory ace Capt Louis H Norley latched onto the tail of another 8th Staffel aircraft and quickly destroyed it. Fellow 10-kill ace 1Lt Ted E Lines claimed three more Fw 190s during the clash;

1Lt Ray S Wetmore downed four Fw 190s in this P-51B in two engagements on May 19 and 24, 1944. His scoreboard details all his victories up to June 1944, and those crosses marked with a "G" in the center denote strafing kills. (USAF)

OVERLEAF
Unteroffizier Ernst Schröder of 5.(Sturm)/JG 300 fights for his life in his Fw 190A-8/R2 on September 27, 1944. His opponent in this duel was 2Lt Robert Volkman of the 376th FS/361st FG, who was flying a P-51B. A full description of this action appears in the text on pages 60–62. (Artwork by Mark Postlethwaite)

When we were bounced from behind and above by 15 Fw 190s, my wingman hollered for me to break whilst I was trying to discard my right external wing tank. When I broke, I was head-on with five Fw 190s and immediately started firing, causing one to burst into flames. I turned to starboard, still trying to drop my tank, as two Fw 190s came under me, heading in the same direction as I was. I got on the tail of the one nearest to me and started firing, and the pilot bailed out.

At this point an Fw 190 closed on my tail and fired at me, hitting me in the tail and wing. My tank finally came off and I was able to maneuver onto the tail of the Fw 190 that had been firing at me. After three orbits, he broke for the deck, with me right on his tail. I fired from 500 yards down to about 100 yards, and saw strikes on his engine, canopy, fuselage, wings and tail. He burst into flames and went into the ground and exploded.

Lousy weather over Germany foiled operations against the enemy on November 14, 1944, but the 359th FG still managed some formation flying for the benefit of the camera. This photograph shows a flight of P-51D-10s from the group's 370th FS, namely *Daddy's Girl* (CS-L/44-14733), flown by Capt Ray Wetmore, *RAYNER Shine* (CS-A/44-14521), flown by Lt Col Daniel McKee, *Mickey the Twist* (CS-G/44-14773), flown by Lt Emory Johnson, and *Blondie II* (CS-S/44-14192), flown by Capt Bob McInnes. (Courtesy of Jack H Smith)

The Fw 190 force again fought back on September 27, when 315 unescorted Liberators of the 2nd Bomb Division went to the Henschel engine and vehicle assembly plants at Kassel, in central Germany. The 445th BG flew into an area a few miles from Eisenach where II./JG 4, IV./JG 3 and II./JG 300, each with a strength of around 30 specially configured Fw 190A-8/R2s boasting heavy armor plate, were maneuvering into their preferred line abreast formation for an attack. From 1003hrs, the B-24s were subjected to a ferocious mauling by approximately 40 Focke-Wulf fighters, the aircraft attacking in three waves.

In less than five minutes the *Sturmgruppen* attacks had decimated the 445th BG, with no fewer than 22 Liberators being shot down in just three minutes, followed by three more in the following three minutes. Staffelkapitän Oskar Romm of IV.(Sturm)/JG 3 destroyed three of the bombers in one single attack. B-24 pilots put out frantic calls for help on the Fighter Channel, and immediately two Mustang groups covering the 3rd Division some 75 miles away near Frankfurt, and the 361st FG, escorting the 1st Division 100 miles distant, came speeding to the rescue. However, six precious minutes were to elapse before the 361st FG could reach the beleaguered 445th BG, and the other two P-51 groups arrived after the enemy had departed.

One of the pilots involved in the subsequent melee between the *Sturmgruppen* Fw 190s and the yellow-nose P-51s of the 361st FG was Unteroffizier Ernst Schröder of 5.(Sturm)/JG 300. He had taken off from Finsterwalde in his Fw 190A-8/R2 "Red 19" *Kölle-alaaf!* ("Up with Cologne!") along with the rest of his *Gruppe*, hell-bent on attacking Eighth Air Force *Viermots*. The unit intercepted the 445th BG formation heading for Kassel, and Schröder downed two of the group's B-24s. There was so much debris in the sky that he closed his eyes because he believed he would run into something.

Below him, ten to fifteen columns of smoke from the explosions of the crashing aircraft rose up through the cloud layer 3,300 ft above the ground. There was burning wreckage everywhere, and the fields were covered with white parachutes. Having descended to low level to make good his escape, Schröder could clearly see crewmen who had bailed out running through the fields;

When I flew over them they stood and raised their hands high. Soldiers and policemen were running towards them to take them captive. Suddenly, a P-51B with a yellow nose (from the 376th FS/361st FG) shot towards me. In the wink of an eye we raced closely by each other on an opposite course. When we had flown by one another, the maneuver began anew, so that we flew towards one another like jousting knights of the Middle Ages. Both of us opened fire simultaneously. The American hit my tail section. My heavy MG 151/20 20mm cannon and MG 131 machine guns failed after a few shots.

Since I could not fire a shot, I began evasive maneuvers the moment the American opened fire so that he could not aim correctly. It was a strange feeling each time looking into the flash of his four 12.7mm guns. After we had played this little game five or six times, I escaped by flying low over the ground. The American turned sharply, but the camouflage paint on my Fw 190 made it difficult for him to find me against the dappled ground.

I landed after minutes of fearful sweating at 1130hrs at Langensala Airport after 90 minutes of flight time. An inspection of my fighter showed some hits in the tail section and a part of the covering of my rudder had been torn off, but the damage was so slight that I could take off again at noon. I landed at 1215hrs at Erfurt-Bindersleben, where my bird had to be repaired in the hangar.

This event made it very clear to me that the Americans had now achieved air superiority, as their fighter escorts were very effective. Indeed, we had only achieved such great successes on this day because the bombers we had attacked were for some reason unescorted.

An Fw 190A-8/R6 of Stab JG 26 has a 21cm mortar round carefully loaded into its underwing WGr 21 "stovepipe" in the spring of 1944. This weapon was introduced in the summer of 1943 in the hope that it would help break up bomber formations. Although a direct hit could have a devastating effect on a B-17 or B-24, the drag and weight associated with the tubes in turn had a detrimental effect on the Fw 190's performance. Most units were therefore reluctant to use this weapon in areas where bombers were escorted by fighters. (Courtesy of Eddie Creek)

It appears that Unteroffizier Ernst Schröder's opponent during this mission was 2Lt Robert Volkman of the 361st FG's 376th FS, who had followed his formation leader, 1Lt Victor Bocquin, down through the cloud cover in pursuit of the fleeing Fw 190s while the remainder of the group continued to escort the remnants of the B-24 formation to the target. During the fight that ensued, pilots from the 376th FS operated singly or in groups of two or three as they chased down the Focke-Wulfs. Bocquin claimed three Fw 190s destroyed and 1Lt William 'Bill' Rockefeller Beyer was credited with downing five. In all, the American fighters and bombers claimed 29 fighters destroyed during the course of this mission (the Luftwaffe officially acknowledged the deaths of 18 pilots).

TARGET GUNSIGHT VIEWS

Introduced in the spring of 1944, P-51 Mustangs were fitted with the K-14 gunsight. Instead of the typical crosshairs one might expect, the K-14 projected a centre dot of yellow light surrounded by six diamond-shaped dots. A gyro computing gunsight, the pilot could preset the gunsight with the wingspan of a target. Once the enemy was sighted the K-14 gave an accurate reading of range and the required lead necessary. Manuals were given to pilots to explain how to use the gunsight and where the diamonds should be placed to ensure a kill. The basic idea was to maneuver until the dot could be placed on the enemy target, using the twist grip on the throttle handle to adjust the reticle of diamonds. The placement of the diamonds depended on the angle of the enemy plane. At ranges of less than 600 feet the diamonds were meaningless. The dot simply needed to be kept on the target with maximum fire. Of course in a dogfight itself it was not as simple as it sounds. In the closing years of the war the skies above the Reich were crowded with airplanes. When engaging the enemy, more than anything, it was crucial not to become a target yourself.

Credited with a total of 18 German fighters destroyed in the air and another three on the ground, the 376th FS had set a temporary record among the fighter groups of the Eighth Air Force for enemy aircraft destroyed by a single squadron on a single mission.

On November 27, II.(Sturm)/JG 300's Unteroffizier Ernst Schröder again took on an overwhelming number of Eighth Air Force "heavies" which were out in significant numbers attacking various transportation targets. He and his fellow pilots, who were part of a large *Gefechtsverband* led by 128-kill ace Oberstleutnant Walther Dahl, were set upon by the now seemingly ever-present Mustangs.

In a series of wide-ranging dogfights over the Halberstadt–Quedlingburg area – the scene of so many Sturm assaults in the past – the *Gruppe* lost seven pilots killed and four wounded. Unteroffizier Ernst Schröder was very nearly one of them. With his trusty "Red 19" having been hit in the rudder, thus making it almost impossible to turn, Schröder was attempting to escape at low level when;

> Suddenly a bare metal P-51, looking brand new, appeared just above to my left. I could clearly see the pilot peering down at me from his large glass canopy. He obviously didn't want to overshoot and get ahead of me so, using his excess of speed, he pulled up and away to port.
>
> I could no longer see him but, expecting him to attack at any second, I nearly dislocated my neck trying to look behind me. When I glanced forward again, the edge of a forest of large trees was filling my windscreen. I heaved back on the stick, but there was an almighty crash as my *"Bock"* tore through the top branches of a huge tree at something over 500kmh (310mph). My cockpit immediately filled with blue smoke as I carefully tried to gain enough height to bail out.

In fact, Unteroffizier Schröder managed to belly land his machine on a nearby airfield. It was a sorry sight. The spinner and wing leading-edges looked as if they had been "attacked with an axe," there were at least 25 bullet holes in the wings and fuselage, and lumps of tree were found embedded in the radiator. It was the end of the road for Schröder's well-known "Red 19" *Kölle Alaaf!*

The Luftwaffe lost more than 50 fighters that day.

Things did not improve come the new year, and on January 14, 1945 the red and yellow-nosed P-51s of the 357th FG based at Leiston, in Suffolk, shot down 60.5 enemy aircraft – a record for any Eighth Air Force fighter group which remained unbeaten through to VE-Day. The 20th FG claimed 19.5 victories that same day and the 353rd FG downed nine enemy aircraft. In all, 161 enemy aircraft were destroyed by VIII Fighter Command units.

Since flying its first combat mission on February 11, 1944, the 357th FG, commanded by five-kill ace Col Irwin H. Dregne, had been credited with 517 victories. No fewer than 42 pilots had attained ace status whilst flying with the group, and its ranking ace, Capt Leonard "Kit" Carson of the 362nd FS, who, on November 27, 1944 had become an ace by shooting down five Fw 190s, added three more kills to his score on January 14, 1945. His first victim was an Fw 190 singled out at the rear of a gaggle flying 20 miles northwest of Berlin;

I closed to about 400 yards, firing a good burst and getting strikes all over his fuselage. I believe the pilot was killed. I went back up to the bombers, looked around for a couple of minutes and saw a formation of about 40 to 50 Fw 190s coming up about 1,000 yards behind us. There were a couple of P-51s nearby, and they broke with me. We met the enemy aeroplanes head-on. They didn't fire but we did.

I opened fire from 600 yards, closing to 200 yards, getting strikes on both wings. The Jerry split-essed for the deck and I followed him down, firing some more and getting additional strikes. At about 18,000ft the pilot bailed out, and I watched his 'chute open. Shortly thereafter, one of my wingmen, 2Lt John F. Duncan, shot down his second Fw 190. This time the pilot did not get out of the exploding fighter. I then fired a burst from 350 to 400 yards at yet another Fw 190, getting strikes. He did a couple of snaps to the right with his belly tank on, and wound up on his back. I fired again, getting more hits on the fuselage. Pieces came off the enemy ship and he began smoking. He split-essed and headed for the deck. I followed him down until he hit, bounced and crashed. The pilot did not get out.

By 1445hrs all the 357th FG Mustangs had landed back at Leiston, and pilots were soon telling their mission accounts to amazed interrogation officers. As the story went up the line to 66th Fighter Wing and higher headquarters, recounts were ordered. However, the score remained the same. Only 13 P-51s and three Thunderbolts had been lost during the great air battle of January 14. JG 300 reported 27 pilots killed and six wounded, while JG 301 had 22 pilots killed and eight wounded. The 357th FG was duly awarded a Distinguished Unit Citation for its exploits on this day.

These *Sturmböcke* of II.(Sturm)/JG 300 were photographed at Holzkirchen in late August 1944. The pilot snatching 40 winks in the shadow of 'White 5' is Unteroffizier Friedrich Alten, who would go down in this machine (Wk-Nr. 681366) near Kassel on September 11. (Courtesy of John Weal)

WILHELM HOFMANN

Wilhelm Hofmann was born on March 24, 1921 in Reichelsheim, in the Oderwald region of Hessen. A future stalwart of JG 26, he joined the unit upon the completion of his operational training with Ergänzungsjagdgruppe West on June 11, 1942. Unteroffizier Hofmann was duly assigned to Fw 190-equipped 1./JG 26, and gained his first victory on October 11, 1942 when he shot down a No 64 Sqn Spitfire IX near Cassel. On December 9 Hofmann's Fw 190 A-4 (Wk-Nr. 5617) suffered engine failure in flight and he was forced to crash-land near Watten. He suffered severe injuries in the accident, and was hospitalized for four months.

Hofmann eventually returned to 1./JG 26 on March 31, 1943, by which time the unit had been posted to the eastern front. Here, he shot down a Soviet LaGG-3 fighter on May 14, thus doubling his score — this was his sole claim in the East. Hofmann's unit returned to the West in the autumn, and in September 1943 Feldwebel Hofmann transferred to 10./JG 26. However, his stay with this *staffel* was short, for he was serving with 8./JG 26 by the time he claimed his third victory (a No 132 Sqn Spitfire IX) on October 18.

On February 29, 1944, recently promoted Leutnant Hofmann was appointed *Staffelkapitän* of 8./JG 26, and on March 15 he recorded his tenth victory. Included in this tally were two Mustangs — the first, an RAF Mustang I from No 2 Sqn on January 28, 1944, and the second a P-51B from the 363rd FG on March 8. Hofmann was to enjoy considerable success over Normandy following the Allied landings, being awarded the Deutsches Kreuz in Gold on July 22 for 26 victories (including six Mustangs). He brought his score to 30 on August 20 by claiming two USAAF P-47s.

On October 22 Hofmann suffered an injury to his left eye in a ground accident when the bolt in a dismounted aircraft machine gun suddenly closed whilst he was examining it. Unperturbed, the ace continued to fly combat missions whilst wearing an eyepatch! Leutnant Hofmann was awarded the Ritterkreuz on October 24, by which point he had claimed 40 victories — remarkably, a quarter of this tally was comprised of RAF Mustangs and USAAF P-51s.

On January 1, 1945, Hofmann led 8./JG 26 on Operation *Bodenplatte*, attacking Brussels-Evere airfield. Two weeks later he assumed command of 5./JG 26, whilst also retaining control of 8./JG 26. However, on February 15 8./JG 26 was disbanded and he became the permanent leader of 5./JG 26.

Hofmann led a formation of eight Fw 190s from Drope on a *Jabojagd* mission in the Wesel-Bocholt area on March 26, 1945, and the formation soon encountered USAAF B-26s near Münster. He expertly led a bounce of the RAF Tempest V fighter escort, shooting down a No 33 Sqn aircraft for his 44th victory. However, during the ensuing confusion Hofmann went missing, and it was later determined that he had been shot down in error by his wingman and crashed between Hasselünne and Flechum. The ace had managed to bail out, but he was too low for his parachute to deploy properly.

By the time of his death, Wilhelm Hofmann had been credited with 44 victories achieved during the course of 260 missions. Some 43 of these successes had been gained on the Western Front, and included five four-engined bombers, 13 P-47s and ten P-51s.

STATISTICS AND ANALYSIS

In the spring of 1943, the growing strength of VIII Bomber Command began to exert great pressure on the Jagdwaffe in the West, and this would only continue as the war dragged on. By the end of the year the Luftwaffe, unhappy with the relatively small number of bombers being shot down, had drastically revised its tactics. On December 20 the fighter force made its attacks from dead ahead, or "12 o'clock level." Closing speeds of around 550mph made it difficult to keep targets in effective firing range for more than a split-second, and there was always the fear of collision at the back of the German pilots' minds. Larger attacking formations, and simultaneous attacks by fighters, rather than in trail, were now also being used.

Fighter *geschwader* perfected their head-on approaches in early 1944, increasing the angle of attack to ten degrees above the horizontal in an effort to increase the time targets were in effective firing range. This approach was soon dubbed the "twelve o'clock high" attack by USAAF bomber crews. As before, the best chance of knocking a bomber out of formation was to kill the pilots in the cockpit.

Luftwaffe fighter pilots observed a points system in combat for aerial successes, and these were in turn converted into various awards. An *Abschuss* or shoot down of a *Viermot*, or *4-mot* (a four-engined bomber such as a B-17, B-24, Lancaster, Halifax or Stirling), earned three points, while a *Herausschuss*, or separation, was worth two. A pilot who finished off an already shot up four-engined bomber was awarded one point for *endgültige Vernichtung*, or final destruction. Damaging a bomber sufficiently to force it from its combat box was recognized as being more

Hauptmann Alfred Grislawski, *Staffelkapitän* of 1./JG 1, is seen here with his Fw 190A-7 'White 9' (Wk-Nr. 430965) at Dortmund in January 1944. Surviving the war with 133 kills to his credit, he claimed 17 victories (including two P-51s) while leading 1./JG 1 in 1943-44. This particular Fw 190 was lost in combat with USAAF heavy bombers on 22 February 1944 while being flown by Gefreiter Alfred Martini of 2./JG 1. (Courtesy of Eddie Creek)

difficult than the final destruction of a damaged straggler. Shooting down a fighter was also worth one point while a *Herausschuss* or *endgültige Vernichtung* did not carry any points.

Decorations were awarded after points totals were reached. One point earned the recipient the Iron Cross Second Class, and three resulted in the awarding of the Iron Cross First Class. Forty points were needed for the Ritterkreuz, although this varied in practice. Of course this system often led to overclaiming.

One of the most effective anti-bomber tactics devised by the Jagdwaffe in late 1943 was the employment of specially-armored Fw 190s to attack boxes of "heavies" from behind in tight and massed formations. Major Hans-Gunther von Kornatzki is acknowledged to have been the driving force behind this concept, which he put into practice in the *Reichsverteidigung* (Defense of the Reich) with Sturmstaffel 1 ("Storm Squadron 1") between October 1943 and April 1944. Flying the Fw 190A-6 (from February 1944 the A-7 and from April the A-8) *Sturmjäger* ("Storm Fighters"), Sturmstaffel 1 became operational from Dortmund in January 1944.

Although during the ensuing months the unit managed to notch up a fair number of *Viermot* victories whilst operating from Dortmund and Salzwedel aerodromes, losses from defensive fire and American escort fighters were also very heavy – at least 14 of the volunteer pilots had perished by April 1944. Incorporating the remains of Sturmstaffel 1 as its 11th Staffel at Salzwedel airfield in April 1944, IV./JG 3 became IV.(Sturm)/JG 3, practicing the same 'Storm' tactics in the *Reichsverteidigung*.

Fw 190A-8/R1 to R6 variants that followed were similar to the A-6/R1-R6, but the A-8/R8 used by the *Sturmgruppen* had a specially armored cockpit. The *Rammjäger* notched some notable successes against American bombers, with the most successful mission being flown on 7 July 1944 when 32 "heavies" were destroyed for the loss of just two Fw 190A-8/R7 fighters. It was an isolated success, however, and after D-Day, many Fw 190 *gruppen* were reduced to flying ground attack sorties against invading Allied forces.

Major Heinz Bär claimed 221 victories in World War II, and he was the leading P-51 destroyer in the Fw 190, with 11 kills to his credit. (Courtesy of Eric Mombeek)

Late in the war the *Tagjagd* or day fighter pilots were badly trained and hastily thrown into the battle against all odds, and only a handful survived in the lethal skies over the Third Reich. Unteroffizier Fritz Wiener, born on July, 24 1925, was one of the young replacement fighter pilots who joined the *Reichsverteidigung* at the end of 1944;

The young pilots, who had only limited chances to survive in air combat, were misused as "cannon fodder". In 1944 half the German fighter force consisted of combat experienced pilots about three to four years older than myself, whilst the rest were inexperienced replacements. The majority of the latter category had only minimal flying hours in first-line fighters, and no combat experience at all. It was not uncommon for replacement pilots to arrive in the frontline having never flown the Fw 190, or having practiced take offs and landings in formation. Firing the MK 108 cannon and MG 151 machine guns prior to going into combat was also a rare feat.

Combat tactics, combat formation flying and combat maneuvering in formation were entirely new tasks to be learned. All of this was taught to replacement pilots during a period of just two months, with periodic restrictions on flying time because the Luftwaffe's fuel supply was already becoming limited to even combat units. Although there was no shortage of aircraft in which to fly, the build quality of some of these machines left much to be desired due to poor workmanship and sabotage in the production plants in Poland and Czechoslovakia.

USAAF FIGHTERS IN THE ETO/MTO 1942–45

Type	No of Sorties	Lost in Combat	Enemy A/C Claimed Destroyed in Air	Enemy A/C Claimed Destroyed on Ground	Combat Missions Loss Rate Per Sortie
P-51	213,873	2,520	4,950	4,131	1.2%
P-47	423,435	3,077	3,082	3,202	0.7%
P-38	129,849	1,758	1,771	749	1.4%
P-40	67,059	553	481	40	0.8%
Spitfire	28,981	191	256	3	0.7%
A-36	23,373	177	84	17	0.8%
P-39	30,547	107	14	18	0.4%

LEADING Fw 190 ACES WITH P-51 VICTORIES IN THE ETO

	P-51 kills	Overall score
Oberstleutnant Heinz Bär	11	221
Oberleutnant Wilhelm Hofmann	10	44
Hauptmann Emil Lang	9	173
Oberleutnant Konrad Bauer	7	68
Oberstleutnant Walther Dahl	6	128
Oberleutnant Hans Dortenmann	6	38
Hauptmann Siegfried Lemke	6	96
Oberleutnant Peter Crump	5	31
Oberleutnant Gerhard Vogt	5	48
Leutnant Wilhelm Mayer	5	27

The Jagdwaffe based its highly valued Sturm units primarily at airfields to the south and west of Germany's major industrial complexes in a vain attempt to defend these key locations from daylight bombing raids undertaken by the USAAF's Eighth and Fifteenth Air Forces.

This Fw 190A-8 was one of 60 German aircraft downed by the 357th FG on January 14, 1945 – the record one-day score for the USAAF in the ETO. The fighter's right gear leg has dropped open, indicating that the Focke-Wulf's hydraulic system has been holed – this was a sure sign that the aircraft was doomed. The canopy has also been jettisoned, and the pilot can be seen hunched down behind the windscreen. This photograph was taken by the camera gun fitted into the wing of a P-51D. (National Archives)

LEADING USAAF P-51 MUSTANG ACES IN THE ETO

	Aerial Victories
Maj George F. Preddy (P-51B/D)	23.833 (+3 in P-47D)
Lt Col John C. Meyer (P-51B/D)	21 (+3 in P-47D)
Capt Leonard K. Carson (P-51B/D/K)	18.5
Maj Glenn T. Eagleston (P-51B/D)	18.5
Maj John B. England (P-51B/D)	17.5
Capt Ray S. Wetmore (P-51B/D)	17 (+4.25 in P-47D)
Capt Clarence E. Anderson (P-51B/D)	16.25
Capt Donald S. Gentile (P-51B)	15.5 (+2 in Spitfire & 4.33 in P-47D)
Capt Donald M. Beerbower (P-51B)	15.5
Capt Richard A. Peterson (P-51B/D)	15.5
Lt Col Jack T. Bradley (P-51B/D)	15
Maj Robert W. Foy (P-51B/D)	15
1Lt Bruce W. Carr (P-51B/D)	15
Capt William T. Whisner Jr (P-51B/D)	14.5 (+1 in P-47D)
Capt Henry W. Brown (P-51B/D)	14.2
Capt Wallace N. Emmer (P-51B/D)	14

AFTERMATH

VIII Fighter Command veteran Capt Pete Hardiman was a great fan of the P-51 Mustang, which he flew in the ETO in 1944–45;

My only complaint, was that we did not get P-51s a year sooner. Even Herman Göring knew he was licked when he saw B-17s escorted by P-51s over Berlin. My first meeting with the Mustang was in March 1944. Compared to any fighter I had seen or flown before, she was beautiful. I fell in love at first sight. Finally, I knew that North American had kept its word and given us the best fighter ever designed. The P-51B could be everything a Spitfire could (except climb), and much more. It was the most honest aeroplane I ever flew, possessing no bad flying habits. The threat of liquid-cooled engine vulnerability to combat damage with the Merlin was only true if all coolant was lost immediately – some nursing was quite possible if the oil cooling remained intact, particularly in colder air. I personally nursed mine home some 600 miles from Frankfurt with a coolant leak. Going to Berlin and back was not the most comfortable way to spend one's day, but doing it in a P-51 negated the discomfort somewhat. Nevertheless, we could not stand or straighten our legs upon returning to base. Long high-altitude flying on oxygen saps one's stamina, but having the P-51 Mustang to do it in was a life saver.

Fellow ETO Mustang pilot Lt Col Bill Crump was just as enthusiastic;

The P-51D was the answer to a fighter pilot's dream. A wonderful flying machine, it possessed an excellent view of the world around, was a fantastic gun platform and was designed to combat all enemies at any distance from base. With a well trained pilot aboard, the P-51D was a match for any and all piston-engined fighters. When you shove 61 inches of manifold pressure to that Rolls-Royce Merlin, and that enormous four-bladed propeller starts chewing on the atmosphere up ahead, you receive an undeniable communiqué. You are going somewhere aloft, and fast. Then when you start maneuvering this creature and become aware of the positively sensual balance of the controls, you just might find yourself humming a love song. Every airman worth his tin wings nurses a sneaking suspicion he is a natural as a fighter pilot, and those of us who were blessed enough to fly the Mustang were certain of it.

MUSTANGS OUTSIDE THE ETO

In spring 1942, 500 of the A-36A version of the P-51A were built for dive-bombing. Fitted with wing-mounted dive brakes, these aircraft were the first USAAF Mustangs to see combat, equipping two groups in Sicily and Italy in 1943. The first P-51A group was the 54th, which remained in Florida for replacement training, while later A-models went to Asia for the 23rd and 311th FGs and the 1st Air Command Group, flying their first missions in the China-Burma-India theater on Thanksgiving Day 1943.

In the early months of 1944 US Mustangs began operating in Burma in support of airborne troops attacking Japanese lines of communication 200 miles behind the Assam–Burma front. P-51Bs were also introduced in the Fifteenth Air Force in Italy at this time, and on May 5, 1944 RAF Mustangs operating from eastern Italy destroyed the Pescara Dam through dive-bombing.

Green-nosed P-51B/Ds of the 359th FG's 369th (IV) and 370th (CS) FSs head back to East Wretham, in Norfolk, in formation on November 14, 1944 after their escort mission had been scrubbed due to bad weather. Each VIII Fighter Command group was usually assigned 48 aircraft, which were in turn split between three squadrons. (USAF)

The RAF was second only to the USAAF in the number of Mustangs it used in World War II. The Mustang III (British equivalent to the P-51B/C) entered service with the RAF in February 1944 when it began equipping No 19 Sqn at Ford. The first 250 ordered had the older, hinged cockpit canopy. With a maximum speed of 442mph at 24,500ft, the Mustang III was more than a match for German propeller-driven fighters in 1944, and could operate far over the continent with the aid of drop tanks. Mustang IIIs continued to escort medium and heavy bombers on the Channel front into the autumn of 1944, before moving into liberated airfields in France and serving with the 2nd Tactical Air Force (TAF) as fighter-bombers.

Mustang IIIs and Vs equipped 18 RAF squadrons in the UK and western Europe and six units in the Mediterranean theater. At the end of 1944, Mustangs serving with the 2nd TAF were withdrawn and rejoined Fighter Command in the UK, and Mustangs of Nos 11 and 13 Groups continued to escort USAAF Eighth Air Force daylight raids until war's end. Some Mustangs were still serving with Fighter Command as late as November 1946. Only 280 P-51Ds were supplied to the RAF (which designated the aircraft the Mustang IV) because of the USAAF's demand for long-range fighters in the Pacific.

The Mustang's "long legs" made it a natural choice for bomber-escort and fighter sweeps across the vast Pacific theater. Following the capture of Iwo Jima in February 1945, P-51Ds began escorting B-29 Superfortresses in the USAAF's brutal assault on the Japanese mainland. With external tanks giving a total of 489 US gallons of fuel, an 11,600lb P-51D had an absolute range of 2,080 miles and an endurance of 8 1/2 hours.

On April 7, 1945, P-51Ds penetrated Tokyo airspace for the first time. That same month production of the P-51D ended with total Mustang numbers standing at

The remains of Maj "Kit" Carson's P-51K-5 44-11622 *Nooky Booky IV* rots in a German scrapyard near Nuremberg in the summer of 1945. This aircraft was declared war weary and reduced to salvage following service with the 357th FG at Neubiberg (R-85), near Munich, as part of the Occupation Forces in 1945–46. (Jack Rude)

15,484. Of that total, some 5,541 were on strength with the USAAF on VJ-Day. The D-model's replacement, the lightweight P-51H, appeared too late to take part in operations in Europe, but a few of the 555 H-models built served in the Pacific towards the end of the war, although none saw combat. On November 9, 1945 the last production Mustang (a P-51H) was built, although several more development aircraft appeared beyond this date.

Postwar, Mustangs served with at least 55 air forces. Some were operated by the newly formed Strategic Air Command until 1949, and the P-51K was withdrawn from service in 1951. When the Korean War began in June 1950, many of the 1,804 Mustangs (now designated F-51s) in service with the Air National Guard (ANG) or in storage were recalled to active service. Within a year the USAF had ten F-51 wings, and three of these saw considerable combat in the first 18 months of the conflict in Korea, as did Mustang units of the South Korean, South African and Australian air forces committed to the war.

The final F-51Ds serving with the USAF's ANG were retired in March 1957, although examples remained in frontline service with Central and South American air arms well into the 1970s.

Fw 190

During World War II, some 13,367 Fw 190s, 6,634 Fw 190 fighter-bomber and close-support aircraft and 67 Ta 152 reconnaissance and high-altitude fighters were produced by Focke-Wulf and other German aircraft manufacturers. A tropicalized version for use in the Mediterranean theater saw the Fw 190A-4/Trop built with

This Fw 190A-8/R2 (Wk-Nr. 681497) was flown by 5./JG 4's Gefreiter Walter Wagner during Operation *Bodenplatte* on January 1, 1945. Attacking the Allied airfield at St Trond, in Belgium, on what was only his third ever combat mission, Wagner was forced to land near his target when the engine of his fighter cut out after being hit by groundfire. (Courtesy of E Creek)

tropical filters and a rack for a 550lb bomb under the fuselage. The A-4/R6 had no MW 50 power-boost equipment but could carry a WG 21 rocket missile tube under each wing, and the A-4/U8 was a long-range fighter-bomber variant, which carried a single 1100-lb bomb under the fuselage and a 300-litre drop tank under each wing. Armament was reduced to two 20mm MG 151 cannon in the wing roots.

In 1942 1,850 Fw 190A-3 and A-4 fighters and 68 Fw 190A-4/Trop and A-4/U8 fighter-bombers were delivered to the Luftwaffe. Fw 190A-5/U2 versions equipped with anti-glare shields and flame-shrouders over the exhaust outlets were used with limited success at night on *Wilde Sau* (Wild Boar) operations – a form of freelance nightfighting with the aid of searchlights. The Fw 190A-5/U3 was a fighter-bomber variant carrying two 550lb bombs and one 1100lb bomb.

Perhaps the last word on the Fw 190 should go not to a German aviator but to British test pilot Capt Eric Brown, whose vast flying experience on all manner of military types has allowed him to recognize the true greatness of the Focke-Wulf fighter;

Several fighters were to display the hallmark of the thoroughbred during World War II – aircraft that were outstanding to varying degrees of excellence in their combat performance, their amenability to a variety of operational scenarios, their ease of pilot handling and their field maintenance tractability – but none more so than Kurt Tank's remarkable creation sporting the prosaic designation of Focke-Wulf Fw 190, but dubbed more emotively, if unofficially, the *Würger* (Butcher-bird) by its designer himself.

BIBLIOGRAPHY

Boiten, Theo and Martin W. Bowman, *Raiders of the Reich – Air Battle Western Europe: 1942–1945* (Airlife, 1996)

Boiten, Theo and Martin W. Bowman, *Battles With the Luftwaffe* (Janes, 2001)

Bowman, Martin W., *Great American Air Battles of World War II* (Airlife, 1994)

Bowman, Martin W., *Four Miles High* (PSL, 1992)

Brown, Capt Eric, *Four of the Finest* (RAF Yearbook, 1975)

Brown, Capt Eric, *Wings of the Luftwaffe* (Airlife, 1987)

Cora, Paul B., *Yellowjackets! The 361st Fighter Group in World War II* (Schiffer, 2002)

Caldwell, Donald J., *The JG 26 War Diary Vol 2* (Grub Street, 1998)

Caldwell, Donald J., *JG 26 – Top Guns of the Luftwaffe* (New York, 1991)

Campbell, J., *Focke-Wulf Fw 190 In Action* (Squadron Signal, 1975)

Davis, Larry, *P-51 Mustang In Action* (Squadron Signal, 1981)

Duxford Diary 1942–45 (W Heffer & Sons, 1945)

Fairfield, Terry A., *The 479th Fighter Group in WW2 in Action over Europe with the P-38 & P-51* (Schiffer, 2004)

Gotts, Steve, *Little Friends – A Pictorial History of the 361st FG in World War 2* (Taylor Publishing, 1993)

Green, William, *Warplanes of the Third Reich* (Doubleday, 1972)

Gruenhagen, Robert W., *Mustang – The story of the P-51 fighter* (Arco, 1976)

Hall, Grover C., *One Thousand Destroyed* (Morgan Aviation Books, 1946)

Held, Werner, *Fighter! Luftwaffe Fighter Planes and Pilots* (Arms & Armour Press, 1979)

Hess, William, *Osprey Aviation Elite Units 7 – 354th Fighter Group* (Osprey, 2002)

Ivie, Thomas G., *Osprey Aviation Elite Units 8 – 352nd Fighter Group* (Osprey, 2002)

Jarrett, Philip, *Aircraft of the Second World War* (Putnam, 1997)

Johnson, Air Vice Marshal J. E. "Johnnie", *Full Circle – The Story of Air Fighting* (Pan, 1964)

Long, Eric F., *At The Controls* (Airlife, 2001)

Lowe, Malcolm V., *Osprey Production Line to Frontline 5 – Focke-Wulf Fw 190* (Osprey, 2003)

McLachlan, Ian, *USAAF Fighter Stories* (Haynes Publishing, 1997)

McLachlan, Ian, *USAAF Fighter Stories – A New Selection* (Sutton Publishing, 2005)

Miller, Kent D., *The 363rd Fighter Group in WWII – In Action over Europe with the P-51 Mustang* (Schiffer, 2002)

Mombeek, Eric, *Defending The Reich – The History of JG 1 'Oesau'* (JAC Publications, 1992)

Morgan, Len, *Famous Aircraft Series – P-51 Mustang* (Morgan Aviation Books, 1963)

Morris, Danny, *Aces and Wingmen* (Neville Spearman, 1972)

Nijboer, Donald, *Cockpit: An Illustrated History* (Airlife, 1998)

Nowarra, Heinz J., *The Focke Wulf 190 – A Famous German Fighter* (Harleyford, 1965)

Obermaier, Ernst, *Die Ritterkreuzträger der Luftwaffe Jagdflieger 1939–1945* (Verlag Dieter Hoffmann, 1966)

O'Leary, Michael, *Osprey Production Line to Frontline 1 – North American Aviation P-51 Mustang* (Osprey, 1998)

Olynyk, Frank, *Stars & Bars: A Tribute to the American Fighter Ace 1920–1973* (Grub Street, 1995)

Powell, R. H., *The Blue Nosed Bastards of Bodney* (Privately Published, 1990)

Price, Alfred, *Luftwaffe Handbook 1939–1945* (Ian Allan, 1986)

Priller, Josef, *JG 26 – Geschichte eines Jagdgeschwaders. Das JG 26 (Schlageter) 1937–1945* (Verlag Kurt Vowinckel, 1956)

Scutts, Jerry, *Osprey Aircraft of the Aces 1 – Mustang Aces of the Eighth Air Force* (Osprey, 1994)

Smith, Jack H., *Osprey Aviation Elite Units 10 – 359th Fighter Group* (Osprey, 2002)

Smith, J. R. and Antony, Kay, *German Aircraft of the Second World War* (Putnam, 1972)

Speer, Frank E., *The Debden Warbirds – The 4th Fighter Group in WW II* (Schiffer, 1999)

Spick, Mike, *Luftwaffe Fighter Aces* (Ivy Books, 1996)

Wagner, Ray, *American Combat Planes* (Doubleday & Co, 1982)

Weal, John, *Osprey Aircraft of the Aces 9 – Focke-Wulf Fw 190 Aces of the Western Front* (Osprey, 1996)

Weal, John, *Osprey Aviation Elite Units 1 – Jagdgeschwader 2 'Richthofen'* (Osprey, 2000)

Weal, John, *Osprey Aviation Elite Units 20 – Luftwaffe Sturmgruppen* (Osprey, 2005)

Wells, Ken, *Steeple Morden Strafers 1943–45* (East Anglian Books, 1994)

Wood, Tony and Gunston, Bill, *Hitler's Luftwaffe* (Chartwell, 1979)

GLOSSARY

Abschuss	Confirmed victory in air combat
Abshüsse	Confirmed victories in air combat
Abschussteiligung	Contribution to a confirmed air-combat victory
Alarmstart	Scramble
BG	Bomb Group
Deutsche Kreuz im Gold	German Cross in gold
Einsatz	Operational flight
Erganzungsgruppe	Replacement or complement wing
ETO	European Theater of Operations
Feindberuhrung	Contact with an enemy aircraft
FG	Fighter Group
Flak	(Flieger Abwehr Kanonen) Antiaircraft Artillery
FS	Fighter Squadron
Führer	Leader
Geschwader	Roughly equivalent to three RAF wings, comprising three or four *Gruppen*
Gruppe	Group containing three or four *Staffeln*, designated by Roman figures, e.g. IV./JG 26
Gruppenkommandeur	Commander or Captain, a *Gruppe* command position rather than a rank
Herausschuss	Claim for a bomber shot out of formation
Horrido!	Tally ho!
Jagdbomber	(*Jabo*) Fighter-bomber
Jagdgeschwader	(JG) Fighter wing, includes three or four *Gruppen*
Jagdwaffe	Fighter Arm or Fighter Force

Jäger	Fighter
Kachmarek	Wingman
Kommandeur	Commanding officer of a *Gruppe*
Kommodore	Commodore or Captain, a *Geschwader* command position rather than a rank
Luftwaffe	Air Force
Maschinen Gewehr	(MG) Machine gun
Maschinen Kanone	(MK) Machine cannon
PTO	Pacific Theater of Operations
Reflex Visier	(Revi) Gunsight
Reichsluftfahrtministerium	(RLM) German Air Ministry
Reichsverteidigung	Air Defence of Germany
Ritterkreuz	(Träger) Knight's Cross (holder)
Rotte	Tactical element of two aircraft
Rottenflieger	Wingman, the second man in the *Rotte*
R/T	Radio telephony
Schlachtgeschwader	(SG) Ground attack wing
Schwarm	Flight of four aircraft
Schwarmführer	Flight leader
Schwarzemänner	Groundcrews or 'black men', so-called because of the color of their tunics
Stab	Staff flight
Staffel	Roughly equivalent to a squadron, designated sequentially within the *Geschwader* by Arabic figures, e.g. 4./JG 1
Staffelkapitän	Captain, a *Staffel* command position rather than a rank
USSTAF	United States Strategic Air Forces (Eighth and Fifteenth Air Forces)
Viermot	Four-engined bomber
Wilde Sau	'Wild Boar', freelance nightfighting tactic over bomber command's targets
Zerstörer	'Destroyer', Bf 110 fighter aircraft
Zerstörergeschwader	(ZG) Heavy fighter wing (Bf 110 or Me 410 twin-engined fighter)
Zweimot	Twin-engined bomber

INDEX